THE LAST PLACE I LOOKED

A STORY OF HOPE, INSPIRATION, TRANSFORMATION, AND RESTORATIVE JUSTICE

HERBERT D. BLAKE

EDITED BY DIANA S. BAUMBAUER

BALBOA
PRESS

A DIVISION OF HAY HOUSE

Balboa Press books may be ordered through booksellers or by contacting:

Balboa Press
A Division of Hay House
1663 Liberty Drive
Bloomington, IN 47403
www.balboapress.com
1-(877) 407-4847

Because of the dynamic nature of the Internet, any web addresses or links contained in this book may have changed since publication and may no longer be valid. The views expressed in this work are solely those of the author and do not necessarily reflect the views of the publisher, and the publisher hereby disclaims any responsibility for them.

The author of this book does not dispense medical advice or prescribe the use of any technique as a form of treatment for physical, emotional, or medical problems without the advice of a physician, either directly or indirectly. The intent of the author is only to offer information of a general nature to help you in your quest for emotional and spiritual well-being. In the event you use any of the information in this book for yourself, which is your constitutional right, the author and the publisher assume no responsibility for your actions.

Any people depicted in stock imagery provided by Thinkstock are models, and such images are being used for illustrative purposes only. Certain stock imagery © Thinkstock.

Printed in the United States of America.

ISBN: 978-1-4525-8184-2 (sc)
ISBN: 978-1-4525-8185-9 (e)

Balboa Press rev. date: 9/27/2013

TABLE OF CONTENTS

DEDICATION

There have been several editions of this love story released since Herb originally conceived of the idea of putting his experience to paper. This is the final edition and is dedicated to the memory and legacy of my beloved husband, Herbert D. Blake and his tireless work in hope, transformation, spirituality, and Restorative Justice. It is an honor that I present to you this lasting message from a man who by his very presence made magic happen when he walked into a room and shared fully his love and joy with each and every one of us.

With Much Love and Many Blessings
Diana Baumbauer

PEBBLES . . .

I once heard a marvelous story about Three Nomads who made camp for the night and were just settling in when a bright light came down from above. The nomads promptly got on their knees to honor their celestial visitor and to hear what it had to say.

After a moment the light spoke, "Go out, gather all the pebbles you can find – fill your saddle bags, and in one day's journey you will be happy and you will be sad." Then the light disappeared.

The nomads, still on their knees, looked at each other curiously. They were disappointed with the message. Each thought a Light from heaven would bring a message of how to live forever, or how to find the wealth of the world, or how to heal illness.

Instead, all it said was: "Pick up some pebbles."

Disappointed though they were, the nomads agreed to obey the Light and gather up some pebbles before retiring for the night.

The next day, at the end of a long journey, when the nomads were about to turn in for the night one of them remembered the pebbles. Reaching into their pockets for the two or three pebbles they had saved, the nomads discovered to their surprise and joy, the pebbles had turned to diamonds!

And they were happy – just as the Light had said. Yet when they remembered the other part of what the Light said, "...fill your saddle bags," they were sad. So the Light's prophecy had come true.

The moral of this story for all of us is to never underestimate the people, lessons, or ideas that have the potential to enrich our lives. They may seem as insignificant as "pebbles" today, but throughout the course of our lives, we will visit places that we haven't been before. We will also need skills, friends, and information we never knew we needed.

Therefore, none of us can afford to ignore any pebble that God puts in our path; no matter how small it appears in our present perspective - because today's pebble will be tomorrow's diamond.

FOREWORD

I am going to share with you a story about a most incredible man and his transformation in the most unlikely place.

Part of this story, actually the end, which I share now at the beginning, is how I met this man, fell in love and committed my life to him.

Although our time together was short, the challenges we faced brought us closer together and finally opened up my heart to what he meant when he said he chose me to be his partner for life, and that his love for me was always and in all ways.

Through his daily experiences, Herb taught me what it means to trust that when we are loved we are never abandoned on our path to remembering who we are in the eyes of God.

Herb and I first met at the California Endowment in Los Angeles, California, where he was taking a class in grant proposal writing. I was there for a lunch date with a friend who was also in the same class as Herb. She invited me back to the class for the afternoon session. As a grant writer myself in a past life, I was eager to hear about new information the teacher was sharing with the class. Because I was a guest and not a paying student, I sat in the back of the room as unobtrusive as I could make myself, not intending to participate or be part of class activities.

But as luck (or God) would have it, he spotted me anyway.

For me, Herb immediately stood out from the rest of the class. His easy way of communicating with the other students and the teacher was insightful and inclusive of everyone. He was charming as well as self-effacing with a quick smile that could warm the coolest of hearts.

As part of the training, the students were sent to the computer lab for additional hands-on experience using the Internet to search for potential funding sources. Herb insisted I sit next to him and share his computer terminal. So, I showed him what I knew about researching possible funders and surprised myself when it dawned on me that I was starting to like this guy.

By the end of the day we had exchanged contact information on the pretext of possible funding opportunities for him. He said he was with the Office of Restorative Justice for the Catholic Archdiocese in Los Angeles and this would help him out tremendously. He didn't tell me he was a volunteer there until later.

It was a couple of weeks after that initial meeting in February 2009, that we had our first date. We met for lunch at Homegirl Café, part of Homeboy Industries, not far from the California Endowment. I hadn't sat down but a few minutes when he said he had something to tell me. This is how he put it:

"I have something to tell you and ask you. I'll understand if you don't want to continue our date after you hear what I have to say, but I just got out of prison. I don't have any I.D., I don't have a car; and I don't have a job. Is that a deal breaker?"

After a very long pause, I said, "We'll see."

This little voice inside told me to stay and hear him out. I had no where else to be for the rest of the day, so we spent the rest of that very bright and sunny afternoon at Elysian Park by Dodger Stadium getting to know each other. Life is full of second chances.

That chance meeting at the California Endowment and our subsequent date developed into a wonderful and loving relationship, culminating in not one but two weddings. The first a civil ceremony performed shortly before my departure to the East Coast for a temporary position with the federal government, July 11, 2009, and a full Catholic wedding the day after Christmas, December 26, 2009.

It was no easy task for Herb to adjust from being inside prison for 23 years to a world that had changed significantly in the time he was away. Cell phones, ATM bank cards, and the wonders of the Internet were just the beginning of the learning curve that was almost vertical. He was like a sponge absorbing everything he could reach for and teaching himself what he needed so he could connect to people in this new world of social media, instant communications and high-tech magic.

One of the life lessons Herb learned early and certainly shared with others while he was inside was that there is a proving ground you must go through before you can reach your goals; whether that is getting a job, reuniting with your children and family or just surviving day to day on the outside, you have to be willing to do whatever it takes to build your credibility with those you intend to interact with.

This takes time and patience, faith and a lot of love and support from whomever you call your support system. Whether you are coming home from a physical prison, or struggling to free yourself from a self-imposed prison, you cannot do this transition alone and expect to succeed.

When I met Herb he was newly released from prison, but he was also volunteering at the Office of Restorative Justice. Later on when he wrote this book, he was actively involved in the community through his volunteer work. He facilitated victim/offender reconciliation workshops at Homeboy Industries, was a regular speaker at Loyola Law School, and was a co-chair for the Re-entry committee for the Violence Prevention Coalition of Greater Los Angeles and Long Beach Work Task Force. He had built quite a network of resources and people in the field of social and juvenile justice. Each person he came into contact with he embraced and called "friend". Within less than two years his friends spanned the globe and he invited them to join him on his Internet radio show, Path To Justice, to share their stories of spirituality, restoration and social justice. At the time of his death on January 8, 2012, he was preparing his curriculum for his workshops in forgiveness and conflict resolution.

As is true for all of us, Herb's path was not easy or smooth. Sometimes this path was very hard for him, and he would despair over what he saw as failures on his part and believed he had lost sight of his core values and beliefs. It would have been easy for him to do something stupid to violate his parole and go back inside where he understood the rules. But faced with the real possibility of losing his wife and home, as well as the faith and trust many others had placed in him, he dug in, renewed his belief that God was still there with him and moved forward.

To those challenges, Herb would tell me over and over to trust and have faith that everything would work itself out. And, I have to admit—it did. "Always in God's time, not ours," he would say. He taught me to be grateful for each day and all that it held. Our evening meals were graced with gratitude to God regardless of what the day had brought us.

Herb would tell me, "I have to go where God leads me and I have to give 100%, of my focus to the task, because God doesn't start working until I've given my all. The Divine doesn't kick in until 101%. If I only put in 85% of what is expected of me, I can pray all I want but I'll go wanting. From zero to 100 percent is all my territory. It's that part of my task that relies on my 'natural' abilities. God's Jurisdiction is the Super-Natural; the realm that begins right after what is humanly possible."

Faith is the willingness to ignore space and time and trust that whatever it is we want in our lives will appear at the exact time we need it. All we have to do is hold on.

Faith is a practice not an automatic attribute. We must practice faith so our belief in the things not seen get stronger than the things we see. Life allows us the opportunity to focus more on the obstacles so we see the problem more clearly than we see the solution. And when there is no solution readily apparent that's when faith is the only viable solution to overcoming the obstacle. Faith is the food and water that sustains us across the desert of hopelessness.

Through his transformation Herb didn't have to understand the why of anything, because he just knew God would always be there to guide him to where he was supposed to go.

Although Herb is no longer with me in the flesh, he lives on in the continuing revelations of each day. I am constantly and pleasantly surprised to remember his gentle reminders to trust and it will happen. When we come from a place of fear and put the power of our lives in the hands of others, we are not free. We agree to react to the dictates of others rather than respond from a place of love and awareness. As long as we know deep within our heart that we are truly loved beyond anything tangible our needs will always be met. All we have to do is be aware and the miracles will happen.

AUTHOR'S
ACKNOWLEDGEMENTS

In this book I only mention a few of the people who helped me on my journey to where I am today. I didn't speak about the following, and must at least mention them here: Diana, my wife, Doc, Mrs. Carter, Mrs. Thornton, Cheryl, Al, Dr. Frank, Ray, "Machine Gun" Tony, JudithAnn, Nancy, Terri, Cora, Mrs. Clark, Annie Graham, Ms. Ledesma, Lucky Cruz, Mel Feryance, Dan Crowley, Fr. Mike Kennedy, Fr. Joe Spieler, Sr. Mary Sean Hodges, Rita, Amalia, Vicky, Deacon Doug, Pastor Roy Davis, The Holy Cross Group, Jorge, Sexto, Lorraine, Mary, Jo Ann, Aba Gayle, George, Seth... and the list could go on and on.

I believe I have learned to live my life in a way that conveys my gratitude for all they have done to help me discover who I really am— they all deserve to have the Best Friend I can be.

INTRODUCTION

When I first set out to write this book I had no idea how difficult it would be to put a few thoughts on paper. I estimated I could have the entire project completed in a week or two. I had to revise that estimate to a month, and then finally to "it will take as long as it takes."

Much of this book I wrote sitting in my car in public parks and grocery store parking lots with my body twisted so I could type on my laptop that I balanced precariously on the passenger seat. On a good day, I might find a spot at the public library and work relatively undisturbed until closing time. On a bad day I would sit in my hot, rented room, drenched in sweat, trying to get a word, sentence, or paragraph just right.

I've written other things, all of them fiction, so I could "make it up as I went along." Now, however, I was telling a story that really happened, so I had to pay attention to chronological order and the truth. It turned out to be one of the biggest challenges of my life; yet after I started, I couldn't stop until it was complete. It is said that everyone has at least one book in them. Here is mine. I hope you enjoy it.

I give my energy to educating, illuminating and comforting those who are looking for a way to find a relationship with God and a way out of a nonproductive lifestyle.

~ Herb

CHAPTER ONE

THE BEGINNING—
MARCH 13, 1986

I had pulled into a small parking lot in a Hollywood strip mall. It really wasn't much of a mall, as there was only a drug store, a clothing store, and a Laundromat positioned in a horseshoe configuration with a small parking lot that accommodated about eight cars. I maneuvered head first into a parking place next to the Laundromat.

It was a rather inconspicuous space so I could have my morning eye opener: a bottle of cheap wine to keep my throat moist while I smoked a wake-up joint. It was barely 7:00 AM, but time had stopped holding any meaning for me. I was "on the run" and every minute of every day seemed the same.

Drinking and using drugs were ways for me to combat the panic and despair of my situation. I had considered leaving town, but I had nowhere else to go and no money to get there. I felt fortunate to have had enough to buy wine that day.

I opened the chilled bottle and braced myself for the shock of the first drink when I heard the screech of tires behind me. I glanced up into my rear view mirror and my heart stopped. There were police cars everywhere. The uniformed officers were spilling out of their vehicles with well-organized precision, guns drawn, crouching behind open doors in readiness for whatever happened next.

"You, in the car," a hoarse voice boomed over a loudspeaker, "Keep your hands where we can see them."

For a brief instant I considered turning up the bottle for one last swig, but I thought better about making any move other than the one I had been ordered to do. I didn't want my movement to be misinterpreted as resistance. I sat stock still, both my hands tightly gripping the steering wheel, awaiting further instructions. I didn't have to wait long.

"With your left hand, open the car door. Exit the vehicle hands first and lay face down on the ground." That voice sounded so rehearsed it could have been a recording.

I did as I was told, and once I was lying face down on the cold asphalt the regiment of cops swarmed over me, pinning each of my arms and legs while simultaneously searching everywhere I could possibly hide a weapon. I was handcuffed, pulled to my feet, and asked,

"What is your name?"

I did what any self-respecting criminal would do – I lied. "Mi nombre es Alfredo Garcia. ¿Qué quieres? No hice nada."

The Spanish response threw them off for an instant, but one of the cops came back from the car with a photograph and the ruse was over as quickly as it had begun.

"Not today, Mr. Blake," the cop said, "You are under arrest for first degree murder. You have the right to remain silent…" I didn't hear the rest. I was too preoccupied with making up a story that would let me walk away from this nightmare.

I was marched over to one of the black and white cruisers. One of the cops opened the door while another pushed my head down so I wouldn't injure myself getting into the back seat. I guess I should have been afraid, or sad, or angry, but I felt none of these things. The emotion I remember having was relief - relief that the running was over.

I had no idea then that the end of one thing was the beginning of something far greater than I could have ever imagined.

Looking Back

I had a great childhood, a troubled teen period, and a wild adulthood. I didn't think of myself as a bad guy. I just believed in having more than my share of fun. Unfortunately, a major part of that fun was "using." It wasn't just drugs and alcohol, which I consumed in excess, but using people, places, and things as well. I'm sure the people who cared about me knew that my lifestyle would eventually end up in tragedy.

I know, because they reminded me often that I was headed for trouble.

Regrettably, I was too caught up in what I wanted to listen to anyone. As a result of my blind self-absorption, on February 19, 1986, I shot and killed a man. My reasoning for committing the ultimate crime seems trivial now, but at the height of my ego-driven madness it all seemed to make perfect sense.

He had disrespected me, and therefore had to pay. Ironically, I didn't mean to kill him, yet taking a loaded gun to emphasize a point never has a happy ending. I know that now, but I didn't think of it then.

After sixteen months in jail, going through one phase of trial after another, I pled guilty to a lesser charge of second-degree murder. I was given a sentence of Fifteen Years to Life. Three weeks after sentencing I was on my way to prison.

In retrospect, even though the legal process took almost a year and a half, it seemed like only days between the shooting and my arrival at Folsom State Prison.

CHAPTER TWO

FOLSOM

I arrived at Folsom on the prison bus from Los Angeles County Jail along with 45 other men who had violated the law - maybe not to the extent that I had, but enough to warrant being sent to prison.

It was mid-July, and the temperature was well over a hundred degrees. The thick, long-sleeved cotton jumpsuit I had worn in transit for the 425 miles from L.A. to Folsom seemed to amplify the heat.

Once at Folsom, all the men who had gotten off the bus, including me, were made to stand in a shaded cement area of the main yard while we waited to be issued our prison gear. I couldn't help but notice that there were no other inmates anywhere. The exercise yard was completely empty, but never having been to prison before I didn't give it a second thought.

One of the other new arrivals, who was familiar with the routine, asked the inmate who was issuing us our bedding, "Hey, where is everybody?" Without looking up from what he was doing the man replied, "There were a bunch of stabbings last week, so they locked everyone down."

The first man nodded as if he understood. I looked around at the empty yard as the man's words echoed in my head, "A bunch of stabbings." I found myself wondering, *"Who got stabbed?" Who stabbed them?" Why did they stab them?"* Last, but certainly not least, I wondered what I had gotten myself into and if I would ever be able to get myself out.

I wanted to throw down the bed roll and prison clothes I was holding and run, but everywhere I looked there was either a huge building or a wall that stood three stories high with ten-foot perimeter fences inside the walls covered with ominous coils of razor wire. To top it off, there were armed guards in towers everywhere, so running wasn't an option. And, as I was to learn very quickly, getting released wasn't an option. I wasn't going anywhere for a very long time.

In those days Folsom was a Level Four Maximum Security Prison. The most dangerous men in the state were housed there. The order of the day was "survival" - not survival to get out - but survival to live another day.

I used to wonder what happened to the guys from my childhood who would beat up kids for nothing, take kids' lunch money, and set cats on fire. I found out. They grew up, did something really awful, and ended up in Folsom Prison.

I was in prison for second-degree murder, but I wasn't a killer. At least in my mind I wasn't. Unfortunately, the law wasn't based on what I thought. A man was dead. I was responsible. End of story.

However, for my own well being I had to pretend I was "public enemy number one." I wasn't so much after the respect that came with being a killer as I was the distance that other inmates kept between themselves and someone they thought might kill again.

I walked around Folsom with that "killer look" for three years. I was frightened out of my mind, but I still tried to convince anyone who looked my way that I was a dangerous person.

Most of the other men hung out with their homeboys when they went out into the yard, guys they had grown up with who held the same set of values. Those alliances and values were at the core of the prison gang culture. Each group had its own area on the exercise yard, and those designated areas were off-limits to outsiders.

Entering the wrong area could have serious, even deadly consequences. Since I didn't belong to any of these groups, I stayed to myself and on the move. I didn't want to accidentally get caught loitering in the wrong place.

About a week after I arrived at Folsom, I was in my four-foot-wide by eight-foot-long by eight-foot-high cell lying on the top bunk, when a huge black man I had never seen before came up to the bars of the cell. For a long time he just stood there staring at me. Prison is no place to show fear, so I stared back at him even though my heart was about to jump out of my chest.

Finally, he spoke. "Yo' name Hubbet?" he asked in mumbled, guttural tone.

It took me a moment to realize that "Hubbet" was his attempt to call me by my given name, "Herbert." When it dawned on me what he was asking, I replied in the strongest voice I could muster, "Yeah, why?"

"Boss Shorty wanna see ya tomorra. At yawd (yard). On da bleachas." Then he left.

At the time I had a cellmate named George. I determined early on that he was a tad slow, but harmless. He weighed close to four hundred pounds, which meant we couldn't both be on the floor of our cell at the same time. When he was off his bunk, George took up all the space.

George lived to eat and he ate whatever he could get his hands on. The regular prison food was bad, but the state lunches they gave us were criminal. In spite of the poor quality of those lunches, George seemed to thrive on them. He would eat his, mine, and anyone else's he could get. I saw George gobble down as many as 12 state lunches in one day.

When George wasn't eating he was sleeping. Therefore, I was surprised when he rolled out of his bottom bunk looking at me and asked, "What do Boss Shorty want with you?"

"I don't know. I don't even know who Boss Shorty is," I replied.

George seemed stunned that I hadn't heard of Boss Shorty, and was all too happy to enlighten me. He licked his lips, and then glanced furtively toward the cell door to see if anyone was lurking about on the tier before he began.

"Boss Shorty runs things in here. He head of the BGF and he probably wants you to put some work in since you new."

As hard as I had tried to know things, I had no idea what George was talking about. However, knowing what this was all about seemed critical. It went beyond general curiosity. I needed to know more, because I was a bit shaken by the black giant that had called me by my first name; and secondly, because I had a creepy feeling that I was in trouble. What kind of trouble I didn't know, but it felt like something serious. So, I asked George the burning questions, beginning with, "What is the BGF?"

George chuckled and responded to my question with a question of his own. "You ain't never heard of the BGF? The Black Guerilla Family! They' the baddest gang in Folsom. Hell, they the baddest gang in the state. They might even be the baddest gang in the world."

Every time George increased his estimation of the "badness" of the BGF his eyes got larger. I could tell I was losing him to exaggeration, so I hopped right in with the next question, "What kind of work does this guy Boss Shorty want me to put in?"

When I asked this question George seemed to come back to earth and gave some thought to his response. "He might want you to kill somebody."

Looking into his dull eyes I could tell that in spite of his handicaps George was serious.

"How does he know who I am? How does he know my first name?" I asked these questions as I simultaneously tried to hide my rising panic.

"He knows everything," George said in a low tone that was almost a whisper.

I felt a sense of relief when he said, "he knows everything." If George believed this guy Boss Shorty was a psychic, then maybe the rest of what he was saying was based on delusion, too.

However, George quickly stole that notion from me when he added, "He gets somebody to bring him pictures of everybody that gets off the bus." At that point I felt sick to my stomach.

"What if I don't want to put work in? What could he do?"

I could swear as I asked this I saw a glint of enjoyment in George's eyes when he said, "He'll send somebody who want to put work in to kill you."

"So, what if I don't go to the yard to meet him?"

I got almost the same response: "He'll send somebody to kill you."

Satisfied that I had no choice, I laid down to ponder my fate. Needless to say, that was one of the longest nights of my life.

CHAPTER THREE

BOSS SHORTY

Most morning yard calls seemed to take forever. After being locked up in a one-man cell with another person for eighteen hours I usually couldn't wait to go outside, and the wait seemed interminable. However, the next morning's yard call came much too soon.

As I took my first steps out of the darkness of the huge granite building where I was housed, into the August sun, it took a few seconds for my eyes to acclimate to the brightness. When I was finally able to see, I saw throngs of bodies milling around the yard, and it suddenly occurred to me that I didn't know what "Boss Shorty" looked like.

I even thought about using that for an excuse for missing our meeting. Then, I remembered he knew what I looked like, and the same sick feeling from the night before crept over me again.

I walked slowly, over to the front of the bleachers that faced the softball field and started looking for someone that might be Boss Shorty. I didn't see anyone who fit that description, but I did see a familiar face – Larry. He and I had grown up together and even though I went to Catholic school and he went to public school, we were friends. We played on the same Little League teams, went swimming at the same pool, and when we got older, we went to the same parties.

I was so glad to see Larry that I abandoned my search for Boss Shorty and raced up the steps to the top level of seats where Larry was sitting.

However, when I got within one or two rows of seats from him two big black guys sprang up and blocked my path. I stood there wondering what to do next when Larry said something to them that I didn't understand and they moved to the side so I could pass. (I later found out his instructions were in Swahili.)

I shook Larry's hand vigorously and asked, "Larry, where have you been? One day you were around and then I didn't see you anymore. You just disappeared."

"I've been here," he said in a tone that implied that 'here' was someplace I should have expected him to be.

He was smiling, but suddenly his smile went away and he was looking at me with a serious scowl, "What are you doin' here? You don't belong here."

I didn't have an answer. One thing I did know was I couldn't have agreed with him more – I didn't belong here. Yet his serious moment triggered a wave of seriousness in me, and the joy I had first experienced when I saw Larry went away. My mind snapped back to the reason I was on the yard in the first place – Boss Shorty. I knew I could trust Larry, so in a hushed tone I asked, "Larry, do you know Boss Shorty?"

Larry burst out laughing. I don't think I had ever seen Larry laugh as hard as he laughed when I asked if he knew Boss Shorty. I didn't see anything funny in what I had asked, so I asked him again. This time there was more urgency in my voice.

"Well, do you know him?" I asked. My impatience was growing quickly into panic.

Larry composed himself long enough to say, "Herbert, I'm Boss Shorty – people stopped calling me Larry a long time ago."

Then, I started laughing. Looking back it wasn't the same kind of laugh Larry enjoyed, but more of a *Thank-God-I-might-not-die-after-all laugh*.

As unexpectedly as Larry's laugh had begun, it stopped and he became intensely serious again.

"Herbert, Folsom is a dangerous place."

I held my breath for the part about 'putting work in.' When Larry was laughing he was the guy I used to know, but now he was serious and I saw his Boss Shorty side. "People are killing and getting killed here every day. Sometimes only a few people know why it happens. Sometimes everybody knows – even the cops," he said.

At this point he paused to survey my reaction to his words. Then he continued, "You don't belong here, but, if you mind your own business and stay out of the way, you'll be okay."

His gaze went from me to the two men who had stopped me when I first came up the steps. They had been sitting on the lower level of the bleachers when I arrived, and had since moved to put me between them and Larry. Larry said something else to them in Swahili.

His words prompted them to stand and move to the side, clearing a path for me to leave. I took the hint - my audience with Boss Shorty was over. I shook Larry's hand one more time, but this time it was different – it was colder and he didn't even look at me. His attention was now focused on the softball game.

I didn't know it then, but I had just been placed under the protective care of Boss Shorty and the BGF.

Larry was right. Folsom was a dangerous place. During my three-year stay at Folsom, a lot of bad things happened: killings, stabbings, and brutality. Most of these atrocities were attributed to BGF members following orders from Boss Shorty and subsequent retaliation from other gangs. I don't know to this day if any of it is true, because I did what Larry suggested. I minded my own business and stayed out of the way.

I had a little help. On several occasions someone would come by my cell and tell me things like:

"Don't go to the yard today."

"Don't come out at dinner time."

"Stay away from the track at noon in-line."

Coincidentally, these warnings always preceded an incident, but because I knew in advance, I was able to stay out of the way.

Boss Shorty might have been a bad man, as far as everyone else was concerned, but my friend Larry was my guardian angel.

CHAPTER FOUR

SOLANO

In 1989 I was transferred to another prison: California State Prison – Solano. I was sent to Solano because my custody had been reduced from level four (maximum security) to level three (medium security).

A little known fact about the legal system in California. Everyone convicted of a crime and sent to prison is given an automatic appeal. No one ever wins. It's just a legal formality. The purpose of these appeals is to shine a glimmer of hope on an otherwise hopeless situation. It takes two or three years to find out the sentence being appealed won't be overturned. It's just enough time to get used to being in prison, so when the appeal is denied it's only one more in a series of disappointments.

It was shortly after I was transferred to Solano that I got the bad news that my appeal had been denied. I didn't take it as hard as I would have a year or two earlier. Since I knew I wasn't getting out early, I resigned myself to doing my time and decided to go to school.

I hadn't gone to school for a long time, so I was a bit intimidated by the thought of returning. However, after weighing the alternatives: working as a janitor or working in the kitchen - I signed up for the most challenging class available: Radiologic Technology.

When I initially walked into the classroom the first thing that jumped out at me was a chart that ran down the length of the wall. It was a progress chart with the names of each course and lesson. Along the left side were the student's names and check marks that represented completion of that particular portion of the course.

Looking at all those courses was almost enough to make me turn around and pick up a mop or an apron. However, I took a deep breath and made up my mind to do my best. The course was supposed to last three years – I finished in five months. I was better at school than I thought.

My course at Solano only covered "theory." In order to be state certified as an X-ray tech I had to complete the clinical portion at another institution. At that time there were no training positions open, so I worked as a teacher's aide in the Radiologic Technology class for about a year until an opening for clinical training was available.

I was being transferred to the California Medical Facility, or CMF, at Vacaville. Solano and Vacaville are right next to each other, so it wasn't a big move geographically.

Vacaville

Vacaville was a much more relaxed environment than either Folsom or Solano, both of which are prisons. Vacaville is a hospital. Since I was training to be an X-ray tech I worked in the clinic with civilian medical staff. Working around civilians gave me an opportunity to experience how it felt to be treated like a human being again. When I was in the clinic I was just another person. When I went back to my dorm I was just another inmate.

I wasn't at CMF very long when I saw a friend that I had known from my Folsom days. His name was Bob, and I could tell when I saw him that he was very sick. CMF is a fully equipped hospital and psychiatric treatment center. I was there to train for my X-ray license, but most of the other men who showed up there were either very sick or had mental problems.

Bob had AIDS. When I saw him, he was being wheeled in on a gurney. I only got to speak to him briefly, but I could tell he was glad to see someone he knew by the way he brightened up when he saw me.

"Blake!" he shouted.

"Bob!" I shouted back with joyful surprise.

Our greeting was simple - the message was in the words we didn't say. I didn't bother to ask what he was doing there. He had the gaunt, emaciated look that I had seen many times. X-ray was a frequent stop for AIDS patients and I had seen the devastating effects of the disease on the human body.

Bob was being transported to the AIDS wing and when he called out my name I noticed in spite of his excitement about seeing a familiar face, he could barely lift himself up.

"What are you doing here?" He asked forcing a smile.

"I'm training to be an X-ray tech."

"I'm…" he said, weak and shaky, "I'm sick," but his eyes said, "I'm dying."

My attention turned from Bob to the porter who was pushing the gurney. "Where are you taking him?" I asked.

"G-2." The porter replied.

He didn't have to say anything else. Everyone who worked there knew G-2 was Hospice - the place where terminally ill inmates were sent to live out their last days.

"Look, Bob, I'm working right now, but as soon as I get a chance I will come to see you." Bob's eyes lit up.

"Okay. Thanks, Blake."

He forced out another smile before the porter took him onto the elevator.

In prison, things are easier said than done, and this time was no exception. Later, when I tried to go into the wing to see Bob, even though I worked in the X-ray department I was still an inmate, and inmates were not allowed on the AIDS wing unless they were a PCS worker. No exceptions.

PCS stands for Pastoral Care Service - a group of inmates who volunteer to sit with other inmates who are dying from terminal illnesses. In order to be a PCS worker I would have to sign up. I never liked to sign up for things because they come back to haunt me, but I had promised Bob I would come to see him, and I didn't want to break my promise. So, I went to the PCS office and signed up to be a Pastoral Care Service worker under the condition I could visit Bob right away.

I was told I could visit Bob whenever I wanted, so I went directly to the AIDS wing. When the officer stopped me at the door I showed him my newly minted PCS volunteer card, and she let me in. When I got to his room Bob was asleep, but I sat down in the chair next to his bed anyway. I couldn't help but feel sad for Bob. He was a good guy. I felt so helpless to do anything of any significance to help him. For all intents and purposes his life was over.

I had only been sitting there for a short time when Bob woke up. It was almost as if he sensed that I was there. We talked, laughed, and reminisced. I don't know who got the most out of that visit - Bob or me.

Looking back, I think I was the one more affected by Bob's situation.

I made it a point to see Bob every chance I could. Each time, even if it was only a matter of a few hours since the last time I saw him, he looked weaker. Yet he seemed to have found the strength to deal with the inevitability of his death, while for me his death represented the truth about my own mortality.

There were times when he would see my sadness and cheer me up with a joke or calm reassurance that he would be fine.

Bob only lasted a few days after I was allowed to visit, but I will never forget our time together. I was blessed to witness the most outstanding demonstration of bravery I have ever seen.

Bob taught me that both life and death are what we make of it. If I were dying I don't know if I could be as at peace as Bob was with his end, but I'd like to think I could.

CHAPTER FIVE

JESSE'S STORY

When Bob died I went back to the PCS office to resign. However, before I could offer up my weak explanation for why I didn't want to be a PCS volunteer anymore, the inmate coordinator, Wes, talked me into seeing one more patient.

"Come on, Blake," Wes pleaded. "This guy's volunteer quit and he's got nobody. Just see him until we can get someone else – he's got full-blown AIDS and needs somebody."

Remember what I said about signing up for things usually coming back to haunt me? I felt that signing up for PCS was becoming a lot more than I had bargained for. I didn't know it then, but my decision would change my life forever.

Jesse, my new PCS client, was completely different from Bob. Bob accepted his fate quietly and peacefully. Jesse, who also had AIDS, preferred to go out the way he lived – scratching and clawing.

During my first few visits with Jesse he didn't bother to acknowledge my presence. He sat propped up in bed and watched TV. The only time he looked at me was when he thought I wasn't looking. I thought his behavior was strange, but my assignment was to sit with the patient and that's exactly what I did, day after day.

Then one day as I was leaving, after we'd spent our fourth or fifth "silent" visit, Jesse spoke.

"Are you coming back tomorrow?"

I was so shocked that he said something I had difficulty finding my voice.

"Uhhh…sure, I'll be back tomorrow. Do you want me to bring you anything?"

"A TV Guide," he demanded.

I nodded that I would fulfill his request, but by then he had already looked away from me and back at the TV set. Now that I think back, I'm not sure if he even looked at me while he was asking for the TV Guide.

The TV Guide was the icebreaker. I continued to visit Jesse every day and gradually he started to open up. He hadn't led a life much different from mine, but the fact still remained that he was dying for his mistakes. I was being allowed to live through mine, and because of that I started to feel ashamed of my ingratitude. Here I was resentful of my life sentence, while Jesse would have given anything to serve his sentence out – no matter how long it was.

Jesse had a sentence of 25 to life. He and a crime partner had robbed a jewelry store, but hadn't gotten away cleanly. During a high-speed chase Jesse crashed the car and his crime partner was killed. There is a law called "the felony murder rule" that states if during the course of committing a felony someone dies, the perpetrator(s) is responsible for the death.

Jesse didn't intend to kill his crime partner, but the law is clear and he was convicted of first-degree murder. It was discovered during the routine screening everyone goes through when entering prison that Jesse had HIV. He never mentioned how he felt when he was first diagnosed, and I don't ever remember Jesse saying he was sorry for what happened to his crime partner. I guess he felt that AIDS was his punishment, so he never expressed remorse for anything. If he had said he was sorry, it most likely would have been for the way his life turned out, not for what he had done.

For the next few months Jesse and I talked about everything. The only thing we never talked about was our plans for the future. Essentially, neither of us was looking at walking out of there, so we limited our conversations to things past and present. Things like: sports, women, children, prison, and the existence or non-existence of God.

Jesse didn't believe in God, or whatever belief he had was stripped away when he found out he had HIV. That didn't stop me from talking to him about spirituality; however. I explained that spirituality isn't about God. It's about the best in each of us that we share with those around us.

He listened, but I don't think he ever really bought into the idea. Yet I believe that spirituality was the basis for our relationship. I never told Jesse I felt that way or he might have stopped speaking to me again.

During the time we spent together we helped each other face our respective challenges. I helped him be strong through his ups and downs. He helped me appreciate life in whatever form it takes. We laughed, cried, and found comfort in our friendship even though we knew it was only temporary.

There came a time when Jesse stopped eating. I don't know if he really couldn't eat prison food anymore or if he had just made up his mind that he didn't like it, so he wasn't going to eat it. In his condition not eating was the worst thing he could do, so I started cooking for him.

I made Jesse promise to eat breakfast and I would bring him dinner. I think my willingness to cook for Jesse was because I didn't eat prison food either. I ate breakfast, but cooked my own dinner most of the time, so cooking for him was only a matter of adding a little more to what I was making. I really think I saw an improvement in Jesse's condition when I started bringing his meals. On rare occasions he would pick at the food I brought. I would coerce him to eat by saying, "If you don't want me to cook for you anymore, just say so."

That would be all the prompting he needed to eat his dinner. I knew his condition was affecting his appetite, but he had to eat and if threats were all that worked, then I was willing to make them to keep my friend strong.

Jesse had a 17-year-old son, "Little Jesse," and whenever Jesse mentioned him his mood would brighten. Little Jesse lived with his mother in Las Vegas, which meant Jesse didn't get to see his son very often. Little Jesse couldn't come alone because he was under 18. The rule is that an adult relative must accompany all visitors under 18, so the only way Little Jesse could visit was if his mother agreed to bring him.

Jesse never said anything good or bad about Little Jesse's mother. I suspect she probably represented a part of the wreckage Jesse left strewn across his pre-prison years. I didn't press him for information. I knew how it was – I had skeletons in my closet, too.

Jesse had shown me a picture of his son, and the first thing that struck me about Little Jesse was how much he looked like Celso, one of my dorm mates. They could have been identical twins. You know how they say everybody has a double? Little Jesse was a carbon copy of Celso.

Eventually Jesse wasn't bouncing back from his setbacks as quickly as he had before. The disease was gaining ground on him, and I could sense his fear. Perhaps it was my own fear I sensed. Jesse was yet another reminder of how thin the curtain is between life and death and how easily one can slip to the other side.

Due to his weakened state, Jesse was usually napping when I dropped in for my afternoon visit. However, this particular day I was surprised to find him wide-awake and glowing.

"Blake!" he shouted, "my son is coming to see me next week!"

"Jesse, that's great!" I said, truly happy that his son was coming and to see him so alive.

"Yeah, and you gotta be here." He said. He emphasized his point by grabbing my sleeve and pulling.

"I'll be here, Jesse," I said. "Where else am I going to go? We're in prison," I playfully added.

We both laughed at my response. Yet he wanted to be sure I understood how important my presence was to him. So he pressed me for a more definitive reply before releasing the grip he had on my sleeve.

"You promise you'll be here?"

"Jesse, I'm here every day," I said.

I could tell my response still wasn't what he wanted to hear, so I added, "I promise."

Jesse grinned from ear to ear and let go of my shirt, satisfied that I would keep my word.

In prison one's word is one's bond, because it's all that's left. If a man breaks his word, no one ever takes him seriously again. It's the Code.

Years later I discovered, to my great disappointment, that keeping one's word was more important inside prison than for those living in mainstream society.

For the next week we had the same conversation. I learned to say "I promise" quickly so we could move on to the next topic. As the day of the visit drew near Jesse traded a brand new Adidas sweat suit for a pair of Air Jordan tennis shoes. He wanted them as a birthday gift for Little Jesse. As I stepped into his room the morning after he had made the trade, Jesse was sitting up in bed waving the shoes and smiling broadly.

"Blake, look what I got for Little Jesse! You think he'll like them?"

"If he doesn't like them you can give them to me," I said jokingly.

He handed me the shoes and we spent the next hour commenting back and forth about the workmanship, the tread, the color (white) and every little detail that made this pair of Air Jordan's better than any other pair of tennis shoes ever made. I went along because I understood that these shoes were special – they were for Jesse's son.

Finally, the big day arrived. Visiting hours started at 8:00 a.m., but Jesse made me promise to be in his room at 7:00 a.m. I arrived promptly in his room at 7. The long hour from 7 to 8 o'clock crawled by, but once visiting hours started the time seemed to fly. Nine, Ten, Eleven, Noon... I tried to distract Jesse with trivial conversation, but as the time advanced he got quieter and more preoccupied with the clock.

Visiting hours were over at 2:00 p.m., and by 12:30 p.m. Jesse had become sullen and non-responsive to any attempts I made to engage him in conversation. I knew I had to do something, so I volunteered to call his son's mother to see what had happened. I got the number out of Jesse's nightstand and went out into the hallway to make the call.

After three or four rings a young man answered. My heart sank – I would have preferred that no one answered. Then, at least there would have been hope. But when someone answered on the Las Vegas end, most likely Little Jesse, it meant that there would be no visit today or maybe any other day.

"Hello," the voice on the other end answered.

"Little Jesse?" I inquired, hoping he would say "no."

"Yeah, who is this?"

"My name is Blake. I'm a friend of your Dad. He's been waiting for you to come see him. What happened?"

Little Jesse's tone changed and his voice trembled a bit.

"My mom was supposed to bring me, but she went out last night and didn't come back."

I didn't know what to say to Little Jesse. Deep inside I was embarrassed to admit that I cared very little at that moment about how Little Jesse felt. My main concern was what I was going to tell his father.

I managed to put together words I thought might comfort Little Jesse. I told him how sorry I was that he couldn't come and I ended our conversation by assuring him that I would explain everything to his Dad. Yet when I hung up I didn't have it in me to go back and tell Jesse his son wasn't coming.

Rather than return to face Jesse, I started to leave the hospital wing, but while I was walking toward the door to the main corridor outside I came up with an idea. As I was leaving the wing I asked the officer who was posted at the door for a special favor. After I explained, she agreed, and I left to go back to my dorm.

I didn't go back to see Jesse until the next morning. As I expected he was extremely upset.

"Where were you?" he demanded.

"I'm sorry, Jesse. You looked so sad that your son didn't come that I couldn't stand to see you like that – so I left."

"But he did come! Little Jesse was here!" Jesse shouted joyously.

He was beside himself with excitement and could hardly get his words out.

"He came late and they wouldn't let him in the room. He stood right out there!"

Jesse gestured toward the large Plexiglas window that shielded the patients inside the dorm from those walking by in the hallway.

"He was smiling and waving." He was beside himself with excitement and had to pause to catch his breath.

"I gave him the shoes. That lady guard took them to him". Jesse boasted.

Then his attention briefly turned from Little Jesse's visit to me. "And you missed it," he scolded.

"Yeah, I guess I did." I said.

"He looked great – just like me," Jesse boasted proudly.

"I know Jesse – I've always told you he looks just like you."

We spent the rest of the evening reviewing Jesse's account of the brief visit from his son. I left after Jesse had talked himself to sleep. When I got back to my dorm, Celso was sitting on his bunk admiring his new Air Jordan tennis shoes. Celso and I worked different shifts so this was the first time I had seen him since the day before.

"Hey, Blake, I went to say 'hi' to Jesse and they let me in just like you said, but they wouldn't let me go into his room."

Celso paused thoughtfully, and then asked, "Where did you say Jesse knows me from?"

"Uh, I forget. I'll ask him again tomorrow," I said, while pretending to busy myself with something else.

"And how come he gave me these shoes?"

The question was merely a formality. Celso didn't care why Jesse gave him the shoes. All he cared about was that he had a brand new pair of Air Jordans, but I answered anyway.

"He said you remind him of his son, so he wanted you to have the shoes."

"I want to go back and thank him." Celso said, still looking at the shoes.

"You can't. They only agreed to let you in that one time – you know the rules."

With a sigh of disappointment Celso offered up an alternative that released him of any further obligation.

"Oh, well, you tell him I said 'thanks,' okay?"

"I'll tell him," I said.

I hated to trick Jesse like that, but whatever punishment God has for deception, I'll accept it willingly. It was worth it to have the opportunity to make my friend's last wish come true.

A few days after the visit I went to see Jesse, but he wasn't there. His bed was made and his TV was gone. I didn't bother to ask anyone where he was – I knew. He was in a better place; probably still smiling because Little Jesse had come to see him before he died and he had a chance to give him the Air Jordans.

I left PCS after Jesse died. Perhaps because I had learned the lesson I had signed up for in the first place. Or, maybe I left because I didn't have enough left in my emotional bank account to cover another loss. Whatever the reason, since Jesse, neither life nor death have held the same meaning for me.

I talk a lot about keeping my word, but one of the most touching demonstrations of honoring a promise came years later from my friend Jimmy. I met Jimmy in a group and we hit it off right away. A few months after I met Jimmy I met his wife Liza in the visiting room and she was as warm and friendly as Jimmy. They were good people and became like family to me.

Jimmy wasn't a lifer and when his sentence was about to come to a close he said,

"When I get out I'm going to come back to visit you."

One thing about prison, men make a lot of promises when they're about to get out, but few ever keep them.

I'm sure they are serious when they make them, but life and freedom get in the way. So when Jimmy swore to me that he would come back to visit, I took it with a grain of salt.

After Jimmy went home I got regular cards, letters, and pictures from Jimmy and Liza. Then, three years after Jimmy had gone home, I got a visiting application from him.

I filled it out, but seriously doubted if Jimmy could get in to see me because he was an ex-convict. As I suspected, his application was denied. Jimmy wrote and asked what he should do.

"Write to the warden," I suggested, not really thinking it would do much good. Actually, I was kidding, but Jimmy was serious. He wrote to the warden.

One day while I was on the exercise yard I heard my name announced over the loud speaker for a visit. I had no idea who it could be, but I rushed in, showered, dressed, and went to the visiting room. I didn't know who I was looking for, so I scanned the crowd for someone I recognized. Then I saw them – Jimmy and Liza, standing there smiling. I couldn't believe it.

"What are you doing here?" I asked joyfully, "I thought they turned you down!"

"I did what you said. I wrote to the warden. I'm off parole and I've been clean the whole time – so I was approved. I had to come to see you, because I gave you my word."

It had been over four years since Jimmy left Folsom, and as I stood there looking at him I was overwhelmed with emotion. I believed he meant what he'd said when he said it, but I never believed he would actually keep his word to come back and see me. I learned a lot that day about Jimmy, myself, and most of all, about keeping one's word.

CHAPTER SIX

MORE VACAVILLE

The next few years were the same as the years that preceded them. I finished the X-ray training, tested for and received a state license. The irony was, once I was licensed as a certified X-ray tech I couldn't work in the X-ray department where I had trained. It was "The Rule." A few years earlier the Housekeepers Union, of which the X-Ray Techs are a part, filed a grievance that the inmate techs were taking their jobs. The union prevailed and from then on no inmates were allowed to work in a prison X-ray department. So, I went to the Neurology Department where I learned how to perform EKG's, EEG's, and Treadmill Stress Tests. I soon learned I couldn't stay there either. After reaching a certain level of proficiency I had to move on.

In prison, whenever an inmate learns a job well they have to move on. Their skill-set is perceived as a threat to institutional security. I guess the general idea is the inmate can use their power for evil as well as for good – so let's move them to another area where they have no power at all and everything they learned can go to waste.

After two years in Neurology, I went back to school again - this time for Computer Application. I could type, but I used the "hunt and peck" method. When I was a boy in school, I thought of typing as a woman's skill. Therefore, I didn't bother to learn something I thought I'd never need to know. Over the years I learned a totally different lesson. Time has a way of changing one's mind about things that one is absolutely sure about in their youth.

So, I changed my mind about typing and whose role it is to be trained in that skill. I was grateful for an opportunity to learn how to type properly, learn computer applications, and be in a setting that didn't attract any undue attention. Even though I hadn't seen Boss Shorty for years I still remembered his advice: *"Mind your own business and stay out of the way."*

I met some very interesting people at Vacaville. Between the regular criminals, the infirm, and the psychiatric cases there was never a dull moment. I also met staff members who were "real people." They believed in a man's merit. They didn't pass judgment on him based on his past. I can honestly say that my restorative process began at Vacaville because of those who treated me like a human being. There is a saying: *When we treat a man as he is, we make him worse than he is; when we treat him as if he already is what he potentially can be, we make him what he should be.*

All people need to be treated with respect to bring out the best in them, and if it doesn't, it certainly brings out the best in the person who treats another with respect.

The atmosphere at Vacaville was so relaxed back then that it didn't seem much different than being in the outside world. This was most obvious in the visiting room. In those days, I was a regular visitor, so I got to know a lot of the other men's families and shared in their struggle to maintain some type of normalcy.

In the visiting room we were like one big family. An example of that came one Saturday morning when I was visiting and noticed a Hispanic woman crying at the next table. A woman crying while visiting with her significant other wasn't that unusual, but this woman was alone except for her two small children. I watched her for a while before I approached and asked what was wrong. Through her tears she said, "While I was in the bathroom changing the baby someone stole my purse. I have no money to feed my children, my husband, or buy gas to get back home."

Telling the story of her dilemma made her even more upset and her tears flowed more freely. I hated seeing her so distressed and I searched my brain for a way to help.

"How much money did you have?" I asked.

She broke off her sobs long enough to say, "Forty... (sob)...dollars."

I gently patted her on the shoulder. "It's going to be okay. Don't worry."

I doubt if she believed me. After all I was not only a stranger, but also an inmate who had no reason to care about her problems.

I knew most of the people in the visiting room, so I felt comfortable going from table to table explaining the woman's situation and asking for donations. Everyone was sympathetic and gave something. By the time I was done I collected more money than the woman had lost.

When I returned to her table, she was still crying and hadn't noticed me moving around collecting money. When I handed her the small stack of bills she was shocked. Before she could ask I explained,

"The people here visiting gave you this money to replace the money you lost."

She looked around the room at the visitors who were waiting to see her reaction. Quite suddenly she jumped up, threw her arms around me and said, "Gracias, señor, usted y tus amigos eres muy amable." (Thank you, sir. You and your friends are very kind.)

She proceeded to go around the room to every table and hug everyone that would accept it. A few minutes later, her husband came out to the visiting room and I could see the woman excitedly telling him the story. He came over to me, shook my hand, and gave me a big hug.

"Thank you for taking care of my wife and children," he said.

"Don't thank me," I said. "Thank <u>them</u>," and I gestured toward all the other visitors. Shouting isn't allowed in the visiting room, but he did it anyway. With a heavy Latin accent he yelled, "God bless you all!"

There are some bad people in prison, but mostly there are good people who have found themselves in situations that made them do some bad things. I never asked anyone what he was in prison for – it wasn't my business. Besides, they were paying for whatever it was. I wanted to appraise the man for who he is now, not who he was once. Before I went to prison I never would have thought about helping that lady or anyone else for that matter. However, prison was changing me in ways I couldn't quite understand. At least not yet.

All the prisoners that came out to the visiting room shared a common problem. We all lived with the knowledge that we were the ones locked up – not our friends, wives, parents, or children. At any time our visitors could decide not to come back and there wasn't anything we could do about it. I've seen hard-core criminals, violent men, break down in tears when they learned a loved one had abandoned them. In most cases the person that left was the prisoner's only connection to the outside world.

I could empathize with the men who had to deal with a loss. I had my own experiences with loss. My favorite uncle died two years after I arrived at Folsom, my mother died six years later, and my wife, at the time, left me three times. By the third time I felt a sense of relief. I didn't have to divide my thoughts between my prison program and whether my marriage would survive until I had served my sentence. I concluded that prison is no place to be married. Marriage only adds to the feeling of powerlessness. A man and his wife should be in a position to mutually support each other, but when one can't help or support him/herself, the balance that keeps a marriage healthy is thrown off. For some men, their marriage is the anchor of their existence, but for others it is a source of continual frustration and anger.

Vacaville was a good place to be, as far as prisons go. During my time there, I helped organize a victim/offender reconciliation group. The group was structured so we could bring men and women inside the prison that had been victimized and they could tell their stories. The object of this sharing was to give the inmates insight into the damage they had done and the pain they caused. It opened the door for inmates to accept responsibility for their actions that ultimately put them right where they were-prison. The healing process happened when the victims listened to the stories of men and their apologies. At least that's how it was supposed to go. In most meetings it was a very powerful and enlightening experience for all concerned.

However, there were also instances when the victims didn't want to heal. Instead they came to the prison to denigrate and accuse, demanding of the men who were there to make amends. Those sessions were ugly. Yet, there was a lesson to be learned there, too – being sorry doesn't mean you will be forgiven. Being sorry only means one has come to terms with the gravity of his/her own actions.

I don't think there is a man or woman serving a prison sentence that isn't sorry. However, there are different categories of sorry. I found that many were sorry for their situation and not for their actions. The ones who were genuinely remorseful didn't just say they're sorry they let their actions be heartfelt acts of contrition.

Chapter Seven

My Life

In 1997 there was a riot at Vacaville, and I was transferred back to Folsom. When I left Folsom in 1989 I had promised myself that I would never go back. Lesson learned: *Never say never.*

By the time I returned to Folsom, I had been in prison for ten years and I still hadn't figured out how I went from being a precocious child who had an innate curiosity for life to the convicted killer other people said I was. I attended Holy Cross School in Los Angeles, California, from the first through the eighth grade. Most of the friendships I established in my childhood and continued to enjoy into my adulthood I forged during my Holy Cross years. I was a straight 'A' student, but found myself under the fiery gaze of one nun or another on an almost daily basis. I wasn't a bad kid – I just liked having more than my share of fun—a recurrent theme in my life.

In spite of my shenanigans, I graduated and was accepted to Mount Carmel High School. In the sixties, going to Mt. Carmel was a very big deal. It was one of the most prestigious Catholic high schools in the nation. To make it even better, I had earned an academic scholarship by scoring in the top four of the 40-plus students who took the entrance exam. It wasn't a real "full ride," but it was a half-tuition scholarship. My grandparents would have to pay the other half. I knew that might cause a problem, but I was in my dream school and nothing else mattered.

I joined the swim team, the band, and the football team. However, as it turned out, even half the tuition was too much for my grandparents to handle. Mt. Carmel's policy was that if a student's tuition payments were not current, he was barred from taking weekly tests or participating in extra-curricular activities – like band, football, and swimming.

Not only that, but in order to keep the scholarship I had to maintain a B+ average. It would have been easy under normal circumstances, but impossible for me to do since I was barred from taking exams. Eventually, I was asked to leave. That was almost 50 years ago, but the memory is still as painful today as if it had happened yesterday.

While I was in grade school I wore the telltale black and white uniform of Catholic school that made me a target for all the public school bullies. I was chased, robbed, and beaten up more times than I can remember. The nuns would say that I was persecuted because I was better than my tormentors. That rationale wasn't much of a consolation when I was sporting a black eye or a swollen lip. Leaving Mt. Carmel meant I would have to go to public school and be in the midst of the people who had made my life miserable for so many years. It was a case of that which I feared the most had come upon me.

When I got to public school, I tried desperately to fit in by doing what I thought would make me like everyone else. I smoked, drank, used drugs, and came to believe that manhood was defined by how many different girls I could sleep with. Most of all, I didn't want to appear too smart, so I let my grades slip.

Eventually, the transformation was complete. Instead of being an "honor student," I became an anti-social underachiever. The good news was: I fit in.

I did every dumb, risky, and foolhardy thing I could think of to prove I was just as bad as I perceived those around me to be. In retrospect, I suspect there were times I over-compensated because I had no real point of reference for what bad really was. I had to rely on my Catholic school perception of what a bad-ass should be. Of course, Catholic school versions of anything were, in my opinion, usually better than or worse than the truth. And as a consequence wasn't much help.

As a result, I drank too much, smoked too much, used too much dope, put myself in compromising positions with women, and fought with little provocation. Usually, I lost – unless my opponent was drunker or had taken more drugs. I was shot, stabbed, hit by cars, and involved in multiple car crashes. Maybe I wanted to die, but I didn't have the courage to do it outright. So, I put myself in worst-case scenarios, hoping I wouldn't survive my stupidity.

As I look back over those dark times, I'm convinced that God always kept me just far enough from total self-destruction so I could survive to fulfill the purpose He had for me. I say that now, but for most of my life I was unaware of God's presence, let alone any purpose He might have for me. I lived my life like a set of Chinese nesting boxes - whenever I succeeded at getting out of one box I found myself in another.

I don't know how, but I made it through public high school, and spent a couple of years in college. However, I felt no enthusiasm for learning anymore. I missed my Holy Cross friends and my Mt. Carmel status. I missed who I used to be.

I left college and worked at one job after another until, when I was 25, I found the perfect job. I started working in Hollywood, California, at a toy store. Actually, it wasn't just a toy store – it was a magical place that transformed me into a salesman. I worked at Hollywood Toys for twelve years selling toys, costumes, make-up, demonstrating magic tricks, and totally immersing myself in the Hollywood culture. In 1984 the owners sold the store and I had to look for other employment. By then, I had developed a penchant for sales, so I pursued a career as a salesman. I did well, and soon I had everything I thought would make me happy: fast cars, women, money, and lots of time to explore how many ways I could get into trouble.

My ultimate fall started gradually with driving under the influence, disturbing the peace, carrying a concealed weapon, and ultimately ended up with a life sentence for 2nd degree murder. Anytime along the way when someone asked me what I was doing, I said, "I'm having fun, enjoying life." It wasn't until much later I realized that my misadventures were neither fun nor enjoyable. Fun things come with pleasant memories, but I was always trying to forget. In spite of the path I had to take to get to the place where I am in life today, I'm happy with who I am. I have heard that we are never given more than we can bear because God loves us. I'm sure that's true, but sometimes I think God loved me too much.

CHAPTER EIGHT

BACK TO FOLSOM

When I got back to Old Folsom in the summer of 1997, it wasn't the same place I had left eight years earlier. First, the security level had been lowered from Level Four to Level Two. In the old days, Old Folsom was Maximum Security and contained the most dangerous criminals in the state. However, a couple of years after I transferred to Solano the security level had been downgraded to Medium Security and that meant the prisoner population changed.

That doesn't mean because the security level was lower that Folsom had changed for the better, it would be more appropriate to say that it was less dangerous and less stressful than before. The killings occurred only once every month or so, instead of every day. The other major change was Boss Shorty had been transferred. Not that I needed him anymore, but it would have been nice to have him around – just in case.

Not only had Folsom changed, but I had changed, too. I wasn't the same person I was when I had arrived at Folsom ten years earlier. I was older, of course, and more savvy to the ways of prison, but something inside me had changed. The person I was when I returned to Folsom had never existed before.

I was still on my guard for any unexpected eventuality, but I didn't feel fearful anymore.

This time around Folsom was a much more inmate-friendly place. There were programs. Before there was almost nothing to do but play cards and dominoes, lift weights, and watch TV. Now there were self-help programs and I jumped right in.

I started attending AA and NA while at Vacaville. In the beginning I attended so I could impress the board when I went to my hearing, but I found a lot of comfort in the fellowship that was at the heart of these meetings. Not very long after I started attending I was elected chairman of the AA group. I was honored, and for the next three years I tried to live up to the responsibility that went with the position. I knew the best way to fulfill my obligation, as chairman was to set a good example. So, I showed up on time, I had perfect attendance, I helped out wherever I was needed, and I practiced what I preached.

Shortly after my arrival back at Folsom I was hired as the Pre-Release Clerk, mainly because of the computer skills I had learned at Vacaville. In retrospect, everything I have done since my decision to turn my life around has had meaning and purpose. I might not have understood what it was at the time, but I learned to trust and to keep moving forward.

The position in Pre-Release required me to facilitate self-help programs for men who were about to be released. It turned out to be a wonderful opportunity for me to learn the skills I would need when it was time for me to leave prison.

Since I was doing a life sentence, the students were curious about my motivation for teaching men who were going home - especially since I wasn't going home myself anytime soon. One student in particular asked me outright, "How can you work with men who are going home and you don't have a date to go home yourself?"

I explained by using an analogy: "If a man sits in a restaurant long enough, he's going to eat because that's what everyone else is doing."

He nodded in agreement.

"And if a man sits in a bar long enough, he's going to take a drink because that's what everyone else is doing."

He nodded again.

"And if a man sits in a barber shop long enough, he's going to get a haircut because that's what everyone else is doing."

Now he was nodding and smiling.

"And if I hang out with a bunch of guys who are going home long enough…" I paused, and he finished the thought.

"You'll go home!" he shouted with excitement, because he understood what I was trying to say. We finished the thought together: "…because that's what everyone else is doing!"

I lived by that philosophy for the next ten years, and I surrounded myself with people who were moving in the right direction – up and out. After years of suffering the consequences of self-destructive behavior, I thanked God for every day I had anywhere, even in prison.

People on the outside think prison is a seething powder keg with unimaginable things going on twenty-four hours a day. The truth is prison is BORING. A lot of the men there are just trying to fill all that time.

One of the most popular pastimes is recounting personal exploits. I didn't go in for that because I believe the more a person tells a story, the more ingrained in his/her personality that story becomes. Therefore, a man who has nothing better to do than tell the same old stories over and over locks himself into those experiences and leaves little room for anything new. It's impossible for a person to change the direction they have been going if they keep retracing the steps to get where they are now. A person has to leave the past in the past and build on the present for the future based on new ideas and new experiences.

In 1999, California Department of Corrections and Rehabilitation (CDCR) conducted a systematic closure of many self-help, vocational, and educational programs. The justification was "Budgetary Constraints." The closures saved money, no doubt, but they also extinguished the hopes and dreams of men and women who needed these tools to change their lives.

There were programs available following the 1999 closures, but the enrollment was limited to a small number of inmates. A lot of men who wanted and needed to participate were excluded. However, there were a few men who found ways to continue to change their lives in spite of the scarcity of programs. They had to be very creative and persistent, but they did manage to improve themselves.

I was fortunate enough to get into programs that kept me moving forward for the next nine years. I don't take credit for the decisions I made to join and attend the various self-help programs. I firmly believe that I was divinely guided to join, participate in, and attend certain programs and groups in order to shape the necessary changes for my mental and spiritual transformation. I had no way of knowing while I was doing these things that each piece was a crucial element of the person I was to become. I stopped questioning the significance of things and just went where I was led. In retrospect, my attitude to keep moving forward was the beginning of the fundamental principal of Faith. My ability to see into the future was so limited that I had trust that God, or as some would have it, my Higher Power, would provide me with answers later if I just did everything I could right now.

I've continued to keep that philosophy with me as part of my life. I believe that I have to go where God leads me and I have to give 100% (whether I want to or not) because God's intervention doesn't start working until I have given my all. The Divine Element doesn't kick in until 101%. If I only do 85% of what is expected of me, I believe I can pray all I want to, but God won't help. From 0 – 100% is all my territory – it is that part of my task that relies on my natural abilities. God's jurisdiction is the Super-natural – the realm that begins right after what is humanly possible. I'm convinced that a lot of people get frustrated with God because they want Him to take up their slack. Yet like the old axiom says: God's job I cannot do and my job God will not do.

Along the way, I became aware that people actually listened to me and were interested in what I had to say. The truly amazing thing was that while I was speaking to a group, an individual, or offering advice, I never knew what I was going to say until I said it – the words just came out. That often put me in an awkward position. I couldn't just talk – I had to listen as well, in case someone asked me about something I said later.

On more than one occasion someone I had spoken with would come up to me later and praise me for something I'd said or advice I'd given.

They'd say, "What you told me really helped. Thank you."

"I'm glad I could help," I would reply, without having the slightest idea what I had said to him.

The most embarrassing moments were when someone would ask me, "Remember what you told me?"

I was stuck for an answer and I'd have to admit that I didn't have a clue as to what I had said. Then, the person would repeat the message that had affected them so powerfully, and I was surprised that I had the presence of mind to come up with something so profound.

In addition to everything else that was happening I had started my dance with the parole board. I had accomplished everything I thought would be expected of me. I was a licensed X-ray tech and had completed a computer application course. I had remained disciplinary-free, had a job offer on the outside, and a place to live. However, the first time I went to the board, I was in the ninth year of my sentence and I was given a two-year denial. That meant I was denied parole, but I would have another hearing in two years. I had convinced myself that I would be given a parole date at my first hearing, but the men who had been to board multiple times tried to tell me not to expect anything. As usual, I didn't listen.

The only redeeming factor about my hearings was the support letters from my friends. At every hearing a board member would read the letters from people both inside and outside of prison – people who believed in me and in my ability to be successful on parole. I was touched by the sentiments in these letters because it had never occurred to me that my friends felt that way about me. Some of them would talk about my leadership qualities, my compassion, my intelligence, or relate a story of how I had helped them. Something I had forgotten.

I sat there feeling both pride and shame as I heard the impact I had on other people's lives. Just hearing the letters eased the sting of being denied parole year after year. I sat there and wondere if my life would have been different if I had felt about myself the way others felt about me. I had no answer.

The one thing I did learn from all of this is that we all have our own path through life. We each have our own experiences we have to experience and learn from to move forward. No matter how much we try to convince ourselves we had no choice in how things went for us, I know now that isn't the case. Our paths may have been laid out for us long before we had any input into our course in life, but the path is secondary to how we travel it – the way we handle our journey in life determines who we are, not the paths we take. The path leads us in the direction of where our talents and abilities are most useful and the road only gets rocky when we try to go another way.

The path I believed I had been placed on had me accept that I might never get out of prison. Just in case I forgot, there was always a parole board member, corrections counselor, guard, or inmate more than happy to remind me there was no guarantee I would be paroled – ever. Based on this bleak prognosis for my future, if I was going to have another chance at being all I could be there was a strong possibility it was going to have to be from behind prison walls.

I started by making amends.

My half-brother Kyle was with me the day I committed the ultimate crime. We were both charged with first-degree murder. I thought we were going to trial together, but in order to get a lighter sentence Kyle agreed to testify against me. I was facing 25 to life if I had gone forward with the trial. So, at the advice of the public defender appointed to me, I pled guilty and was sentenced to 15 to life in state prison. In spite of the fact that I was guilty, I was still angry with Kyle for telling the investigator I did it.

In a case where one co-defendant offers testimony against the other they are separated to prevent retaliation. In a highly unusual move Kyle and I were sent to the same prison. We had very little contact with one another. Ironically, Kyle was a gang member and I wasn't, but that wouldn't have saved him if I had let it get out that he had told on me.

He would've been branded a "rat," and in those days rats were dealt with very severely. But I didn't tell anyone.

Rather than tell someone else and let that person handle it, I convinced myself that revenge would be sweeter if I did it personally – later. In retrospect I realize that I didn't want anything to happen to him because he was my half-brother. All that revenge thinking was my way of denying responsibility for my own actions.

For years I was angry, and would go to sleep nights thinking of ways to get even with Kyle for betraying me.

Then something came over me that I can only describe as a moment of clarity. I started feeling guilty for blaming Kyle for something that I did. I realized I couldn't have expected him to risk getting a life sentence just to cover for me. He only told the truth. It was through my own actions that the truth got me sent to prison.

I knew I had to do something. Kyle's sentence was for thirteen years, and by the time I had my epiphany he had served seven years and was out. So, the only way I believed I could make things right was to write to him and tell him how I felt.

It took me a while to formulate the right words, but knew it would mean nothing unless it was written from the heart. Here is the letter I wrote:

Dear Kyle,

I know you think I'm angry with you but I'm not. I had no right to believe that you would give everything to cover for something I did. I am your big brother and my responsibility was to lead you in the right directions, and I failed both you and myself. The least I could have done was allow you to choose whether you wanted to go with me or not. As a result of my selfishness you lost seven years of your life.

I'm writing this letter to apologize to you for putting you in such an awkward position. You didn't do anything wrong. All you did was tell the truth. If I hadn't done what I did you wouldn't have had to make the difficult choice between life in prison and being honest about what you knew. What I want you to know is you didn't betray me. I betrayed you by getting you into a no-win situation.

I hope you can find it in your heart to forgive me for what I have put you through. Whether you write back or not, I want you to know I love you and I'm sorry.

Your Big Brother,
Herb

After I mailed the letter I felt a huge weight lift from my shoulders. I gained an insight into the importance of forgiveness that hadn't been there before. Forgiveness liberates, whether one is doing the forgiving or is the one being forgiven. Forgiveness only requires that one party be willing to do their part.

Admitting to Kyle that my circumstances were no one's fault but my own was a major breakthrough in accepting full responsibility for my actions. Once I came to terms with my role in the way things went down I set out to be the best person I could be, whether I got out of prison or not.

When I stopped focusing on where I was and started working on who I wanted to be, life got a lot easier. Not only did I start feeling better about myself, but my prison experience also took some interesting and unexpected turns for the better.

CHAPTER NINE

LIFE IS GOOD

A few years before I returned to Folsom, I re-united with my oldest daughter, Shari. She was 30 and I hadn't seen her since she was 12 years old. One day in 1996 I got a letter with a return address that I didn't recognize. When I opened the letter it was from Shari. She was inquiring if I was her father. I was surprised, happy, and sad all at once. I wrote back immediately and confirmed that I was indeed her father and we started corresponding on a daily basis. It was through those letters that we got to know each other again. After a few months of writing back and forth she made arrangements to come up from Southern California to visit me in Vacaville.

When she arrived and I held her in my arms for the first time in almost twenty years. I knew this wasn't just a reunion. It was a miracle.

It was about this same time I got an unexpected letter from someone named "Maggie Kite." This time too, I had no idea who she was until I opened the letter and discovered Maggie Kite was Sister John Thomas, my fifth and sixth grade teacher from Holy Cross whom I hadn't seen for 40 years. We started to write and eventually Maggie came to visit me and continued to visit at least three times a year.

At every visit Maggie brought up things from my Holy Cross days. She would tell me that she always knew I was special, apart from everyone else. At first I felt very uncomfortable when she said this, but I finally realized that she wasn't just making conversation. She believed in me back in school and she still believed in me, even though I was in prison.

One of the goals I set for myself was for Maggie to see me as a free man, but that wasn't to happen. She passed away in April of 2005. That doesn't mean she can't see me. In fact, I'm sure she's there watching and supporting me. It just means she can't cheer as loudly as she would like, but I know she's cheering.

Once Maggie told me she loved me "47 times 47." When I asked her what that meant she said Ann, her oldest daughter who was six or seven at the time asked if Maggie knew how much she loved her. So Maggie asked her, "How much do you love me?"

Ann replied "I love you 47 times 47."

Ann's expression of love was special to Maggie because for a six year-old 47 times 47 was an astronomical number.

Now every time I see the number "47" anywhere I know it is Maggie telling me she loves me.

I read a bible passage in Joel 2:25 that described exactly what I felt was happening in my life. "So I will restore to you the years that the locust has eaten." I felt that my life was being restored and was excited about the possibility of what life had in store for me. I felt that a barrier had been lifted and my life was flooded with all the things my "anti-life" had caused me to miss.

I hadn't told anyone I was in prison for the first five years. I was too ashamed. But, I finally called my best friend Greg. I have known Greg since the first day of first grade at Holy Cross School. We go back almost to the beginning. When I called, the first thing he did was scold me for not calling sooner. Then, he asked how he could visit me. Greg stuck with me from that point forward, and even to this day is only a phone call away.

Greg's reaction to my situation felt amazing, but even more amazing was when my youngest daughter, Auriel, came into my life. Auriel was born the day I fired the fatal shot that sent me to prison. The first time I laid eyes on her, she was two days old. She was the most beautiful baby I had ever seen. As I stood there holding her, the gravity of what I had done weighed heavily upon me. I knew that she would need me for a long time to come, but I wouldn't be able to be there for her. One way or another I knew I would have to pay for the life I had taken.

The day she was born, I was both happy and sad as I looked down on her sleeping form. I wanted to make promises for her future, but I had fixed it so that I didn't know what my own future would be. So I just held her and loved her as much as I could, hoping that the love I gave her at that moment would last her until I was able to hold her in my arms again.

I saw my infant daughter only two more times from behind a protective Plexiglas screen in the visiting room of the county jail. The last time was when she was only three months old, and by then I knew I wouldn't be there to raise Auriel and her two brothers, Herbert Jr. and Brandon. I didn't want the three of them to grow up in Los Angeles without a father, so I asked their mom to take them back to her family in Omaha, Nebraska. I figured Nebraska was as good a place as any, outside of Los Angeles, for my children to grow up.

As the years passed and Auriel was old enough to hold the phone, I would talk to her and she would just listen. I always wrote to her and her mother would read my letters to her. When Auriel learned to write I would get cards and letters from her with the unsteady lettering of a novice scribe. She would send her report cards, pictures, and special awards. She wanted me to be part of her life as much as I wanted to be there for her. We did the best we could under the circumstances.

In 2004, Auriel graduated from high school and was offered several academic scholarships. She chose the University of Southern California, even though she had no friends or family in California. Her motive was clear when the first stop she made when arriving in California was Folsom Prison to see me. She picked USC to be near me.

At Folsom, the visiting room opens into a large fenced patio from which the visitors may be seen as they walk down the sloped road from the main gate. I stood at the farthermost corner of the patio – the one that put me closest to the visitors as they walk past the fence to enter the visiting area gate. I craned my neck to pick Auriel out of the throng of visitors marching in quick-time to see their loved ones. I searched frantically to find the face that I only knew from photographs. Then, I saw her, and the rest of the crowd seemed to disappear into a nondescript halo around my little girl. I could see her eyes darting back and forth searching through the sea of faces on my side of the fence. When she saw me she smiled the biggest, most wonderful smile I have ever seen, and my heart completely melted.

I moved from the corner of the patio to the entrance gate and waited until the more savvy visitors deftly maneuvered their way to the front of the line. When Auriel finally got through the gate there was hardly anyone left in line behind her. Then, suddenly, for the first time ever we stood face to face. It was a tense and awkward moment, but I had made up my mind to make our time together as special as I could. I reached out and pulled her into my arms.

"I love you Princess – I am so glad you came," I said.

She hugged me back and said, "Me, too."

She was there in person. Finally. All my anxiety about this first visit turned out to be not as difficult as I thought it might be. Once we broke the ice with a hug we found so much to talk about we were often talking at the same time. I made it clear from the beginning that she could ask me anything. Auriel didn't ask the typical expected questions like: "Why did you do what you did?" and "Didn't it bother you that I had to grow up without you?"

Instead, she asked:

"Do you have a good memory?"

"Are you good at math and science?"

"Do you like to read?"

I answered, "Yes" to all her questions and she replied, "Me, too," to all my answers.

Our conversation was based on the similarities we shared, and after we had established a slew of things we had in common, Auriel cleared her throat and said, "I've always been different and I never knew why." She paused to phrase her next statement just right, and then said. "Now I know why I'm different - it's because I'm just like you."

I couldn't find the words to respond to that, so I said nothing. After all, there are no words to describe the feeling I had when I saw the pride in her eyes for being just like me.

I've always heard that there is a reason for everything and when I met Auriel I knew the "why" to a lot of things that had been a mystery. I knew why I had worked so hard to be a better person - because being a better person made me a better father.

I realized I had to go away so she could grow up to be a beautiful, smart, funny, self-motivated young woman.

Most prisoners beat themselves up for not being there for their children. They don't understand that their children might actually be better off without them present in their lives, making a mess of their lives too. I have no doubt I would have been more of a liability than an asset to Auriel if I had not been sent to prison. The blessing was that I wasn't present in her life as she was growing up to stunt her growth.

We spent two days together in the visiting room, and by the time we parted we weren't strangers anymore – we were father and daughter.

I learned a very valuable lesson from my little girl: Sometimes the best place to be is somewhere else.

CHAPTER TEN

CENTERING PRAYER

Shortly after my return to Folsom, I met a few men who had started a small meditation and spirituality group. After I met with them and experienced meditation, I felt I had found what was missing in my restoration process. I had read several books on Eastern Meditation and Mysticism that Greg had sent me over the years, and I was excited about an opportunity to put all the things I'd read into practice.

We got together and decided to look for a sponsor so we could make our program official. In prison, the sponsor has to be someone from the outside that is willing to volunteer their time to an inside activity. We were lucky when we found our man, Mike Kelley. Mike had been working with Contemplative Outreach, a Catholic organization that promotes spirituality and meditation. He was delighted that we wanted to form a group and stepped right into the sponsorship role.

Once we were official we could open our small group to the general prison population. First, though, we needed a name, so we voted, and "Contemplative Fellowship" was born. We met every Friday night in the Greystone Chapel, and from the very first meeting there was something truly special about our group.

In other prison activities prisoners had the tendency to gravitate to their own race and form cliques. Contemplative Fellowship was different. Something about the energy that was generated from meditation tore down the racial barriers, and after one or two meetings even the most hardcore members started interacting with men outside their normal circle.

Five years after the group got started we were informed that we needed a clergyman to co-sponsor the group since we were meeting in the chapel. The Catholic Chaplain agreed to sponsor us, but he wanted the name changed from "Contemplative Fellowship" to "Catholic Centering Prayer." I thought the name change would send the wrong message to men who wanted to be part of our group, because when they heard about Catholic Centering Prayer they would think it was only for Catholics.

I was pleased to discover that, after the initial wave of objections, things continued as usual as "Contemplative Fellowship." Most of the men didn't seem to care what the name was. They just wanted to have a peaceful place to share spirituality. No one paid much attention to the ones who kept complaining. In prison there are always going to be those who complain about everything. They complain if things are going one way, and then complain if things go in the opposite direction. I think they just want to make noise, and they don't really care what the noise is about – kind of like some people do in the outside world.

The group went well and grew as the members spread the word about the benefits of Centering Prayer. Frequently, we had outside guests from churches and organizations in the community. They had heard about our meditation group and wanted to see first-hand what a prison meditation group was like.

The most distinguished of these guests was Father Thomas Keating, founder of Contemplative Outreach. Father Keating, a Trappist Monk, spent more than 50 years teaching Centering Prayer.

He visited Folsom on several occasions, met with a handful of the original members, (myself included), and would hold a lecture for the entire membership. We ended each of those evenings with a meditation session led by Fr. Keating, whose presence exudes the spiritual nature of his work. Everyone who attended these sessions came away with the feeling that they had been involved in something very special.

Of all the programs I participated in over the years I can honestly say that Centering Prayer was by far the most life changing and rewarding. After participating in dozens of self-help programs, Centering Prayer made me realize that it wasn't my mind that needed attention – it was my soul. I always had the mental capacity to do almost anything I wanted, but the spiritual aspect of my life - that element that gives and receives love - had been missing for a very long time. I got it back with Centering Prayer.

Centering Prayer wasn't just my salvation, but the saving grace of a lot of men who were searching for meaning in a meaningless environment. During our Centering Prayer meditation Folsom Prison's chapel seemed like the quietest place on earth. The outside visitors who joined us can verify that fact. They felt the peace and energy that was generated in a room of society's outcasts, and they left with a new definition of spirituality.

I, too, found something that made everything in life meaningful – the good and the bad. I found so much inspiration in those sessions, and even though I didn't know what I was supposed to do with my life, I did know that prison was where I was supposed to do it. To my understanding, I knew it was physically impossible to be in two places at once, and therefore prison must have been the right place for me because it was all I had.

My spiritual experience shaped the way I lived the other aspects of my life. I found a joy of living I had never known. I passed my joy along to others who had lost their zest for life. Needless to say, some men thought I was crazy for finding happiness in prison. I recall one young man asking me, "How can you be happy? You're doing life in prison."

What he said was more a challenge directed at me personally than a question.

"Happiness isn't about where you are physically, it's about where you are spiritually and mentally," I responded.

I could see confusion and frustration come over his face.

"What do you mean by that?" he snapped.

Some men in prison present themselves as angry, hostile individuals. Maybe they are angry because of their upbringing or life experiences, or maybe because they are afraid and use their gruff demeanor to hide their fear. I imagine most people were intimidated by this young man's harsh tone, but I wasn't. It was obvious he wanted to know more about finding happiness in prison or he wouldn't keep asking questions. So I continued…

"We create our own happiness wherever we are. If we are unhappy it's not because of where we are, it's because of what we believe. Sometimes we're unhappy because we believe what other people tell us about how we should feel, or we borrow the way we feel from people around us."

We were having our conversation on the exercise yard so I asked him to look around. "How many of those guys do you think are happy?" I asked.

I saw him surveying the faces and postures of the scores of men who milled around us. I didn't wait for an answer because I could tell he was too preoccupied looking around to respond to my question.

"Almost everyone here is unhappy, but not because they're in prison," I continued. "They were unhappy when they were in the outside world. Like everyone else in the world they have something they don't want, want something they don't have, or want to be somewhere they can't go. They're unhappy because they've let someone convince them that they are bad people, and they don't know how to fix it."

I paused for a moment to give him a chance to think about what I said before I gave him more food for thought.

"Prison makes us think that we don't have a lot of choices about who we are or the way we live. Yet we do have choices. When I get up in the morning I can either be happy or sad. If I choose to be sad or angry I'm who THEY want me to be. So I'm giving THEM control over my day. But, if I choose to be happy, in spite of everything, I take charge of my day and that day belongs to me. Do you understand?"

"Yeah, I do," he said slowly. "We're cheating them out of something. Right?"

"Right!" I said.

He seemed so pleased that being happy would cheat "them" out of something that I didn't want to complicate his epiphany with further explanation.

The fact that he would be a better person would come to him later. I was just glad he got it in his own way. I was happy when we started our conversation, and after we had talked I was even happier because I had taught someone else a key to being happy - no matter what. Happiness and spirituality are alike in that it doesn't matter how you get there as long as you let it become your main focus and allow it to transform your life.

I can't remember ever being happy as an adult. There was always something missing. It wasn't until I got to prison and my options were limited that I learned that happiness doesn't come from people, places, or things. Happiness comes from within. The people, places, and things either add or subtract from our natural joy depending on the choices we make.

I had made some bad choices and separated myself from my joy for living. I wasn't chasing happiness – happiness was chasing me and I was running in the opposite direction. Finally, I stopped running and happiness caught up to me in prison - the most unlikely place on earth.

In the beginning, my motive for doing all the right things was to convince the parole board I was ready to be released. Looking back, I really wasn't ready to go anywhere; and fortunately, the board could see that. However, I kept trying to convince them anyway. I tried so hard to trick them into believing I was a good person that I tricked myself into becoming the person I was only pretending to be.

The truth is I never got comfortable being in prison, but I did get comfortable with who I had become. I also became comfortable with my ability to help others become comfortable with themselves too. There is no such thing as the right place and the right time. There is only here and now – and what we make of it.

CHAPTER ELEVEN

FREEDOM

My annual parole hearing was the test of whether or not I was improving as a person. Although the format was the same, each hearing was different. There were always two board members, but never the same two. So every time I went to the board it was like starting all over again. The board members would read my file 15 minutes before I came into the room for my hearing. That meant as far as the board was concerned, my crime was only 15 minutes old – no matter how long I had been in prison. Nothing I had said or done in the previous hearings meant anything. The day of the hearing was always the beginning of a whole new ballgame with a brand new set of board members.

After three or four hearings I knew the post-deliberation speech by heart.

"Mr. Blake, we want to commend you for your accomplishments, and they are many. However, we do not find you suitable for parole at this time."

After being denied parole several times it would only seem natural that I would get discouraged, but I believe in the "Yes Debt," which is based on the principle of Universal Parity: Every positive has a negative to balance it out. So every time I made a request, challenged a situation, or asked a question, if the answer was "Negative," I knew the Universe had an unattached "Positive" waiting to respond to one of my future requests, challenges, or questions. It doesn't work on a one to one ratio, because sometimes I run into a series of No's before I get the Yeses. However, I know the Yeses will eventually come, because they have accumulated in number with each No response. All the Yeses create a "Yes Debt" that the Universe is obliged to pay off sooner or later to maintain a parity balance.

The trick is to remain faithful to the principle – there are times when it seems that the No's will never end and every response is "No!" But, the Yeses will come. I used to feel somewhat glad when I got a "No," especially when it concerned something minor and I had a big event coming up. I knew if I could get as many "No's" out of the way as possible, the odds of getting a "Yes" when it really counted increased tremendously.

In 2006, at my eleventh hearing, I was taken by complete surprise when the commissioner deviated from the usual ending of the post-deliberation speech and said:

"…we find you suitable for parole."

I couldn't believe my ears. After 11 parole hearings, I was finally being granted a parole date! I could hardly contain my joy, and before I left I shook everyone's hand in the boardroom. I felt like I was walking on a cloud.

In California, being found suitable for parole entails a two-step process. The first phase is: the parole board's investigative team checks out all the information the commissioners used to arrive at their decision. That takes four months. If everything checks out, the second phase starts: Governor Review. That takes another 30 days, so all together the parole process takes 150 days.

So I waited, going back and forth between total confidence in my release to doubting that my parole would be approved. On the 150th day I was notified that the Governor had reversed the board's decision, and my release date had been rescinded. I wasn't going home.

The counselor that delivered the news observed me closely for any adverse reaction to the Governor's decision. Some men react badly and have to be locked up until they calm down. The worst part is their behavior is documented and interpreted as an inability to deal with reality. I have witnessed men who had their parole date rescinded cry like a baby or lash out violently at the person who gave them the news. Although the parole review phase is an official process, there is an element of sadistic cruelty involved that can take its toll on a fragile psyche. One hundred and fifty days is a long time to think and re-think the possibilities.

Fortunately, by the last day I had prepared myself for the worst. If good news had come that would have been terrific. But over the years, I had learned that prison isn't a place to expect good news.

I felt badly for the staff members and inmates who had expressed their certainty that I would go home. They felt even worse about the reversal than I did. I especially felt bad for my family and friends who had supported me over the years with letters to the board, and visits, gifts, and encouragement to me.

I was asked time and again, "How do you feel?" "I bet it hurts to find out you're not going home." Actually, it didn't hurt. I had expected nothing and I got nothing. So I was right where I left off – in prison. I spent the next few days apologizing to everyone for not coming/going home. It wasn't my fault that the Governor took my date, yet it was my fault that I was in prison. My letdowns were the repercussions of all the people I had let down in my life.

I went to my Centering Prayer group first, to explain that I was sorry I had disappointed them. I told them, "Maybe the lesson I'm supposed to teach isn't about how to parole with style, but how to accept disappointment with dignity and faith, and that it's all happening for a reason."

I didn't know it then, but I would make the exact same speech to the exact same bunch of men the following year – 2007, when I was found suitable again, only to have my parole date rescinded just like the year before.

When I went to my 2008 board hearing I knew what to expect. The board would find me suitable, and 150 days later the Governor would rescind the date. It was all as predictable as waking up in prison every day.

As usual, I thought I knew all the answers, but God had another plan. When the Governor took my date in 2006, something miraculous happened that demonstrated how wondrous God's ways truly are.

My best friend Greg's godson, Norm, had come to visit me several times and we had become friends. Norm was a Berkeley Law Professor at the time, and after hearing the story of the 2006 reversal he offered to help me challenge the Governor's decision. I hadn't thought to ask Norm because he was a law professor and not a practicing attorney, but I agreed to let him try.

Norm prepared a petition challenging the Governor's 2006 reversal and filed it in state court. It was denied at the first level, so he submitted it on the Appellate level where it was also denied. Ultimately, it was denied in the California Supreme Court and Norm filed the challenge in Federal Court. He had cautioned me in the beginning that the process could take a long time, and he was right.

While all this was going on with my 2006 denial I had been found suitable again in 2007, but the result was the same – the Governor rescinded the parole date again. Norm was relentless, and he filed a petition challenging the 2007 reversal also. It took a while, but the state court didn't summarily deny the petition this time, and instead demanded that the Governor explain why he had rescinded my parole date. The state's justification for taking my parole date was that I presented an unreasonable threat to public safety – even though I had done over twenty years without a single disciplinary action.

The Attorney General's response was unsatisfactory, so the court ordered my immediate release. The state had five days to release me, yet by the time I was notified one of the days had already passed. I was called into the counseling center and the supervising counselor instructed me to take a seat. She looked across her desk at me for a moment before she asked, "What did you do?"

I thought she was accusing me of some rules infraction, so I answered her question with a question.

"What do you mean what did I do? I haven't done anything," I assured her.

"You did something, because we have to let you out in five...uh, four days."

I couldn't believe what I was hearing. After being in prison over twenty years, never knowing when or if I was going home, to hear that I was going to be released in four days was both amazing and a bit overwhelming.

The counselor suggested I keep the news to myself for my own personal security. There have been incidents when a man going home was badgered into a fight and his parole was canceled. Yet I had spent years waiting to go home, and to withhold the good news from the men I had gotten to know like brothers would have felt as if it were an act of betrayal.

One thing about prison news, both good and bad - it travels fast. I had only been out of the counseling center a few minutes when men I knew started approaching me to confirm the news about my release and to wish me the best. Some of the men who came up to me to wish me good luck I didn't know at all, yet I accepted their congratulations as if I had known them for decades.

I'll never forget my last looks at Folsom – even though it was an awful place full of violence and misery, I had spent a lot of good years there, and I could feel myself missing it and the people who I had to leave behind. I was filled with uncertainty and trepidation about what my new life would be like. But I knew that God hadn't brought me through a twenty-three year ordeal just to let me fail.

I didn't make plans for two reasons. First, I had been gone so long I didn't know what plans to make. Second, I had learned to let God handle it, as He has a way of exceeding my expectations.

Those last four days flew by, and before I knew it I was on a bus to a prison closer to Los Angeles – the place where I was initially arrested. It was customary for an inmate to be transferred to the prison closest to the parole area, but because I was under a court order to be released immediately, there wasn't time to schedule a bus to L.A. County. So I was sent to Wasco State Prison in Kern County. From Wasco my parole officer would pick me up and drive me to Los Angeles.

When I arrived at Wasco I discovered that somewhere during the five or six stops between Folsom and Kern County my property box had been misplaced. I only had one box, but it contained everything I needed to make the transition from prisoner to free man, including the civilian clothes I was going to wear. All I had was the paper jumpsuit and a pair of shower shoes that I was issued when I left Folsom. Up until then I had been fairly calm, but losing everything I had in the world pushed me to the brink of my composure. At that moment I drew on the only thing I had left – prayer and meditation. I visualized a happy life in the free world, thanked God that I was getting out, and left the rest up to Him.

I spent a cold night in a temporary cell without a blanket or pillow, but knowing that I was about to be back in the free world kept me warm. The next day, I was returned to a huge enclosed staging area to wait for the parole officer. If there is one thing I learned in prison, it was how to wait, so the three hours it took for the parole officer to arrive went by quickly.

When the parole officer got there, he signed the necessary paperwork to take custody of the prisoner (me) and I was escorted out of the staging area still in my paper jumpsuit and flip-flops. When the parole officer looked up and saw how I was dressed he said, "You can't parole in that!"

"It's all I've got," I replied apologetically. "My property was lost during the bus ride from Folsom."

I didn't know what would happen next, and then the parole officer broke out into a big smile.

"Your box isn't lost. I have it in the trunk of my car. I went to the prison across the road by accident and when I asked for you they said they didn't have you, but they had your box."

He called it an "accident," and some might call it a coincidence, but I call it God responding to my prayers from the night before.

The four-hour ride from Wasco to Los Angeles was spectacular. The farthest I had traveled in 23 years was to a nearby hospital for an MRI and back to Folsom, so my first actual road trip was wonderful beyond words. The scenery was beautiful, and what was even better was I knew at the end of the journey I would be free.

We arrived at the L.A. parole office in the late afternoon and went through the usual procedure: fingerprinting, photos, a review of the conditions of my parole, and finally, FREEDOM. There was only one problem, the transitional house where I planned to live was on the other side of town, and I didn't have a way to get there. I asked the parole officer if he was going to take me and he said he was too busy. He recommended I take the bus. That might have been a viable option for someone who was familiar with where they were, where they wanted to go, and the bus routes, but it had been twenty-three years since I was in Los Angeles and even longer since I had ridden a bus. For all intents and purposes I was in a strange town.

It was 5 o'clock, in December, and the sun was going down. To make things worse, when I walked into the parole office from the car I noticed there were a lot of parolees hanging out in the parking lot. They were the same guys I had left in prison, except they had on civilian clothes.

The parole officer suggested I ask one of them how to catch the bus, but I wasn't anxious to approach them for directions for two reasons: (1) Asking directions implied that I was lost, and, (2) I had the telltale parole box that meant I also had my $200 parole money. At that moment prison seemed safer than the parole office.

I didn't know what to do, so I called Greg. I hadn't talked to him since I had left Folsom, so I had no way of telling him when I would be arriving. Fortunately, I caught him on his way to a meeting that was close to the parole office. When he heard I was out and in Los Angeles he blew off the meeting and came straight to the parole office.

Even though I had grown up in Los Angeles, nothing I had seen since I had returned to the city looked familiar – until I saw Greg. He came striding across the parking lot with a huge grin on his face, gave me a big hug, and for the first time in this whole process I knew I wasn't dreaming.

CHAPTER TWELVE

OUT AND ABOUT

It was nine days before Christmas, December 16th, my birthday, and I was with my best friend embarking on an adventure that would exceed my wildest dreams. Best of all, I was home.

Home is a funny word that means a lot of things depending on who you talk to. Quite a few years before I was released it occurred to me that I didn't have an actual home to go back to. I had no wife or girlfriend; my family (brothers and sisters) hadn't stayed in touch. Shari, my oldest daughter, had her own family, and my other three kids lived in Nebraska.

The reality was I was homeless, and one of the requirements for parole was that I had to have a verifiable residence. That might not seem too difficult, but the residence had to be established before the parole date could be given. Since there was no way of knowing when a parole date would be granted, finding a place to live was an ongoing problem.

I have seen men come to prison with a large support group only to see their "safety net" unravel and disintegrate with the passing years. In 2006, I was fortunate to find a man, John, who ran a sober living house and was willing to hold a room for me. He made it possible for me to have an address to give to the parole board.

When the Governor rescinded my 2006 parole date I contacted John. I explained my situation and the unpredictability of the parole process. Miraculously, John understood and guaranteed me a space whenever I was paroled. When I finally paroled in 2008, I went to John's sober living house, and he had a bed waiting. What began as a business deal for a place to stay turned into another demonstration of how God continued to be in my life through other people.

I could have very easily found myself with nothing and no one, yet in spite of the physical odds to the contrary, things kept getting better. Men and women who have lost their friends and family during their prison sentence often give up on everything else. They feel they have nothing, so there is nothing to lose. They will start to act out in ways that are normally out of character.

Perhaps it is to get the attention that is missing in their lives, or maybe just to let someone know they exist. I have heard that when a person doesn't get positive attention he or she will opt for whatever attention they can get, even if it is negative attention. No one wants to be forgotten.

I was blessed, because my situation was just the opposite of most men who have been in prison. Instead of the time diminishing my support group, my friends and supporters increased. As the years went by, I found myself with more true friends than I had before I went to prison.

I had a lot of time in prison to think about the human condition and what makes people do what they do. I came to the conclusion that our actions are driven by relevance. We all want to feel we matter in some way. Relevance makes one kid go to college while another kid joins a gang. Each does what he or she thinks is necessary to be acknowledged. In search of relevance men and women become saints or sinners. They do whatever it takes to make someone pay attention. I strove for relevance, but never thought my life had much meaning; and therefore, I did something that essentially cancelled my life out.

When I finally became aware of what I had done, I felt even more worthless. It took understanding the way God had been working His Love in my life for me to realize I wasn't a bad person. I was a confused person looking for direction and attention.

Prison taught me how to turn a negative into a positive. I took the stubbornness that had made me cling to a self-destructive lifestyle and turned it into the tenacity I needed to keep going even when the finish line wasn't anywhere in sight. I turned my former inability to follow through into the basis for my faith in God. I was used to giving up, so every night I would still give up, but I would turn the unfinished projects over to God; and in the morning He would give them back with the renewed energy I needed to carry on.

I used the same process with my biggest challenge – freedom. Night after night I would give up on ever being free. Gradually, a sense of calm and certainty came over me. I gave everything about who I am over to God and asked nothing in return. Freedom is the reward for believing that whatever happens is God's Will. My will got me sent to prison – God's Will would get me out. I learned to walk by faith, not by sight, and every step I've taken since has been the right one.

For a long time I found it difficult to believe that good people could genuinely take an interest in me. It was a case of thinking the world saw me the way I saw myself. I did good things, but I could never seem to remember them as well as I could recall the mistakes I made. I wasn't a friend to myself, so I didn't think that anyone else truly wanted to be my friend. I had felt unworthy of friendship all my life, and being a convicted felon reinforced that feeling.

In spite of the way I felt about friendship I always had great friends that I didn't feel I deserved, and friendship wasn't all I thought I didn't deserve. I didn't feel I deserved any of the really great blessings in life. I allowed myself to be satisfied with only the bare minimum, because I couldn't visualize myself with the best life had to offer. I didn't begrudge others their good fortune – I just didn't think that I was one of those people who could be blessed beyond measure.

This attitude caused a real problem in my life, because every time I was on the brink of surpassing my expectations I would find a way to dial things down to a lesser degree – even if that meant sabotaging everything I had built up to that point. It wasn't fear of failure. It was fear of inevitable disappointment.

Fortunately, when my perception of life changed, so did my feelings about friendship. Instead of feeling unworthy of friendship, I became grateful. I came to depend on the men and women who had always been there for me or who had become my friends for support and guidance along the way.

Next, I started working on shifting out of the comfort I found in being an underachiever. I started taking chances, moving out of quiet complacency into areas I hadn't dared to go before. I had always loved to write, but I never showed anyone what I had written. That changed. I started sharing things I had written with others. It was scary at first because I had convinced myself that no one would like what I had written, but I found people did like my short stories, poems, and plays. Not everyone, of course. But I also learned how to accept criticism without letting it be a signal for me to shut down completely.

Life became a complex interaction between who I was becoming and who I used to be. I still pinch myself - not so much because I think I'm dreaming, but to make sure it's really me who is living this fantastic life.

I harbored a lot of regrets, but I came to realize that everything and everyone in life appears for a reason, and maybe not the reason I think. I regretted friendships that didn't work out, but I learned that people come with expiration dates. We don't necessarily know how long our connections are scheduled to last, so we have a tendency to believe that those people with whom we have formed an attachment will be there forever.

Not so. I feel now that some people come to walk with us for a few steps just to keep us from being alone, while others travel with us for a long time to keep us company when the going gets tough. Eventually they take other roads that we can't travel. Then, there are the people who start the journey with us and continue until the end.

The major lesson I learned was that all the people I have had and still have in my life are special and valuable to the creation of who I am and who I will be. I don't regret the ones that have left me because their purpose was fulfilled. Besides, I'm too busy being grateful for what and who I have in my life to regret what I don't have or what I've lost.

As my attitude changed, I gradually moved forward. Soon moving forward became the way I lived my life. At first, I advanced because it was expected of me, and I didn't want to let down those who saw more in me than I saw in myself. I learned how to project confidence even when I wasn't sure about anything. I became confident by pretending to be confident. This was a variation of the ruse I tried on the parole board years before when I pretended to be a good person. Just like then I became the person I was pretending to be. Confidence allowed me to set goals and achieve them without hesitation and doubt. In retrospect, it wasn't so much confidence as it was complete faith that God wouldn't let me fail.

Friendship

I came to the conclusion that we have the kind of friends that we are to others. In order to have good friends, I had to be a good friend. I had to represent all the qualities that my friends possessed for our relationship to be a valid "Friendship."

I'm convinced that it was the miraculous appearance of my special friends that made me take another look at myself. I wasn't quite sure if I was a bad person who had started doing good things or a good person who had done some bad things. I thought about this question for a very long time until I came to the conclusion that I couldn't come to a conclusion.

It wasn't about whether I was good or bad in the past, but the kind of person I am now. "You can tell a person by the company they keep," and if that's an indication of who I had become I was a great guy – because my friends were great people. So great, in fact, that in the beginning my motivation for working hard at being a better person was to be a better friend to the best friends anyone could ever have.

Faith

All my lessons seemed interconnected because on the heels of friendship came a deeper understanding of faith. I came to understand that faith didn't have anything to do with my perception of how life should go or how it unfolded for others.

All the events in our lives are mastered beyond our ability to comprehend. Faith is accepting these events without judging them, and having the trust that God always works to enhance our best qualities. Sometimes things happen differently than we would have liked – faith is the ability to see the best in unwanted situations.

I never really knew what faith was until it was all I had left. I started praying as soon as I fired that gun and haven't stopped since. God hears all our prayers, but I believe it depends on what we pray for that determines His answer. He always answers, and sometimes the answer isn't what we had in mind.

I prayed to God to get me out of prison and He did. It was 23 years later. It wasn't God's fault that it took so long – it was mine. When I asked Him to get me out I didn't say when. Ironically, I was happier about getting out when I did than I would have been if God had granted my request at any other time. He knew that I needed to learn a few more things before I could truly be free, and the lessons were provided in such unique ways that by the time it was over I was convinced that I wasn't sent to prison as a punishment, but because God loved me and protected me until I was able to truly understand.

I believe there is only one kind of faith—faith in God. Faith is the ability to turn something over to a power beyond you, the ego, which will not fail to provide the best result. Faith comes in because on occasion, the outcome of what I pray for isn't what I visualized. For instance, I didn't envision myself being in prison for almost a quarter century. Once I discovered faith, it was no longer a punishment, but rather a mission that I was sure would be over when I had completed the tasks. I didn't know what or how many tasks there were, or how long it would take me to complete them. All I knew was I was doing what God wanted me to do and that was all the information I needed.

I remember someone once asking me, "Do you ever feel like giving up?"

He was surprised when I said: "I give up every night. Then, in the morning I start all over again."

The truth is, giving up would have meant I accepted that I would spend the rest of my life in prison, and I just couldn't do that. So I didn't actually give up – I surrendered. Every night I would surrender the events of that day to my Higher Power, God, and without fail I would awake the next day with a fresh perspective on an old situation.

It worked so well that, even now, at the end of the day, I surrender everything to God and He continues to provide me with fresh perspectives to start a new day. I don't just put my challenges in God's Hands. I give Him my accomplishments, joys, and aspirations as well. All I have left is the peaceful certainty that tomorrow will be a marvelous day touched by God.

CHAPTER THIRTEEN

THE NEW WORLD

I left prison with the anxious anticipation of a toddler on his first amusement park excursion. However, after 23 years the world had changed drastically. Buildings that had been fixed in my memory weren't there anymore. Breathtaking high-rise giants had sprung up in places where simple structures once populated the landscape. I still recognized the street names, but the landmarks I remembered were gone.

I felt like a tourist in a place that once had been my home. However, instead of feeling intimidated I was brimming with eagerness to get started on a new adventure. I was excited by the newness of things. Even the old familiar places looked fresh and wonderful. Most people coming out of prison are happy to have a new life. I was happy to be blessed with a new way of seeing life.

The day after I got out I went to the mall. It was December 17th, eight days before Christmas, and the mall was teeming with shoppers. The stores were adorned with festive Christmas decorations. To add to the gaiety of the occasion, Christmas carols were playing over the loud speakers.

I had heard stories about men who had spent a long time in prison who, when released, were intimidated by freedom. They panicked in crowds and experienced sensory overload in large open spaces like supermarkets or department stores. I wasn't one of those men. I felt like a kid in a giant toy store as I wandered past the glittering storefronts. I had dreamed of this day for too long to feel overwhelmed by its bigger-than-life majesty. It was my first Christmas outside in 23 years, and I wanted to enjoy all of it.

After I had been in prison a while I realized that every day was a gift. I was convinced that God put me there to protect me from myself. At the rate I was going I wouldn't have had 23 years of life left. So if I had not been arrested and sent to prison, my lifestyle would have most certainly been the death of me.

I applied that same "gift" mentality to my freedom. I had just gotten out of prison on a life sentence - an accomplishment that only happens to less than 3% of the men doing a life sentence. Even though I only had a little money and a few clothes that friends had given me, as I stood there in that throng of people doing their Christmas shopping I was thankful for my new world and my new life.

Christmas 2008 was the most remarkable event of my adult life. I was invited to Greg's home for dinner. It was a family dinner and I was included. I sat down at the large table with Greg, his wife Eleana, their son Mason, Eleana's mother Lorraine, Greg's sister Jan, her husband Randy, and their daughter Taylor. After a delicious dinner everyone gathered around the Christmas tree to open gifts. I stood back to watch and enjoy how it feels to be part of a real Christmas celebration. Eleana was reading off the names of the family members who had gifts under the tree. Suddenly she read, "To Herb, From The Family."

She was holding a gaily wrapped box and everyone was looking at me, smiling. I could barely hold back the tears when I realized what was going on. They had bought me a gift!

"I didn't know I was getting a present," I said, trying hard not to let my voice reveal my emotions. "I didn't bring anything for anyone else."

Eleana's smile broadened as she said, "It's Christmas, and everyone in our family gets a present." Even now I get a lump in my throat when I think about that wonderful "Welcome Home Christmas."

Christmas on the outside reinforced the spirit of giving I had learned inadvertently on the inside. When I first went to prison in 1987, holidays were a special occasion. Easter, Fourth of July, Thanksgiving, Cinco de Mayo, and Christmas were all days that I looked forward to. There was always a big meal with things that weren't usually served. On Christmas we even got a special bag of goodies: nuts, candy, sodas, and fruit.

Over the years we got less and less until there was barely any difference between the holiday meal and any other meal. It got so mediocre that I stopped going. Then one year someone I liked invited me to go to Christmas dinner, and out of friendship I accepted. I didn't want the food and it was hard to sit there and not complain and make references to "the good old days." But I looked across the table and there was a man who was enjoying every bite of his holiday meal as if it were one of those fantastic meals I remembered from years ago.

Watching him eat with so much pleasure made me feel ungrateful for even thinking of complaining. It still didn't give me an appetite for the food, but it did give me an idea of how I could make the holiday special – I offered the man my tray.

"Hey, you want another tray?" I asked.

He stopped eating long enough to look at me with suspicion and distrust. I guess the food was so good to him he thought something must be wrong with mine for me to give it away, and he made that clear.

He asked, "Why? How come you don't want it?"

Rather than go into my real reasons I said, "I already ate in the cell because I don't like turkey." It took him a moment to process my response, but then he grinned from ear to ear and took the tray.

It might sound crazy, but that was the beginning of a series of the best holidays I've ever had. Every holiday from that point on I found someone who appreciated what I didn't want, and instead of complaining, I was happy because I made someone's Christmas, Thanksgiving, Cinco de Mayo, or Fourth of July better. I discovered it's not all about me, and happiness can come from making someone else feel like it's their lucky day.

The next few weeks of freedom were a blur of activity as I connected with old friends. I used a formula to determine whether or not I wanted an old friend to be part of my new life. I reviewed the outcome of our last encounter, and if it was positive I felt comfortable renewing our friendship. On the other hand, if our last encounter had a negative outcome I avoided them. I had changed and so had my requirements for friendship. I knew I had to exclude certain people from my life for my own survival, even though in some cases it was a difficult decision.

I met some great people while I was in prison. One of those exceptional people was Ray, a man who had retired from a successful legal practice and chose to volunteer as a sponsor for our Centering Prayer group. We got to be such good friends that he introduced me to his good friend Scott who taught at a law school in Southern California. Scott liked the work I was doing in prison and invited me to do a presentation for his class when I got out. I was extremely flattered by his offer, and I accepted even though I didn't know when or if I would get out. One of my favorite sayings is: "Future events cast backward shadows." So the invitation that Scott made was a "shadow" of things to come.

When I got out I contacted Scott and he and I became the best of friends. I did the presentation at the law school and several others over the next few months.

It doesn't matter where a person returns home from: Iraq, Afghanistan, the hospital, or prison – the result is the same. When the person first gets back, everyone rallies around him/her with gifts and promises. After a while, the excitement of the homecoming diminishes, visitors stop visiting, promises fade, and the phone that was difficult to keep answered goes silent. I was aware that I wouldn't be the center of attention for long, so it didn't come as a big shock when the party was over – with the exception of Scott.

My first big challenge came when I went to the Department of Motor Vehicles, generally known as the DMV, to get a California I.D. card. I thought it would be a simple process because my parole officer had given me a "Temporary ID/Affidavit" with my picture, my height, weight, birth date, and social security number. However, when I took the document to the DMV office I discovered I had been out of the system so long they needed additional proof of identity; i.e. credit card, social security card, or passport. All the things I didn't have because I hadn't needed them for the past 23 years.

"Since 9-11 we are very careful who we give an ID card to," the lady at the DMV informed me in a practiced, professional voice. "There is a lot of identity theft these days," she said, squinting and straining to decipher the parole ID/Affidavit.

"Ma'am, all I want is an ID. I just got out of prison and that paper is all I have," I explained, trying to maintain a calm, even tone.

To help her understand, I reached across the counter and pointed out the first of two sentences on the affidavit that read, "In lieu of an official birth certificate. Information has been verified by the U.S. Department of Justice and the California Department of Corrections and Rehabilitation."

Then I appealed to her logic.

"I know you have to be careful who you give an ID to because of identity theft, but if I were going to steal someone's identity, do you think I would choose an ex-convict?"

I thought I saw the light of serious consideration go on in her eyes, but it went out as quickly as it appeared. She shook her head to both indicate "No" and to clear away any connection that she might have made between what I just said and common sense.

"Nope, you need a birth certificate," she said as she handed back the parole ID and walked away.

An ID card might seem like a small thing, but without it I wouldn't be able to get a social security card, a job, open a bank account, or make any legal transactions. For all intents and purposes I didn't officially exist anywhere except the parole office.

In spite of the inconvenience of being without an ID card, I still managed to make progress. I had a lot of practice dealing with frustration in prison where everything is infinitely more complicated than it needs to be. I didn't take the ID fiasco personally. I knew it would work itself out. I had things to do and I couldn't let one small glitch rob me of my focus and enthusiasm.

The DMV exercise in futility was my first interaction with the bureaucracy of the new real world. For the next five months I went through a series of hoops and setbacks until I got a California ID card. It took a lot of help from my friend Scott, his friend Dan, and a sympathetic judge to finally get it. Everyone, not just people getting out of prison, needs people like Scott, Dan, Greg, Norm, and a sympathetic judge or two to help smooth out the rough patches.

I hadn't found a job, so I started volunteering my time at the Office of Restorative Justice, an organization that works with victims, offenders, and the families touched by crime.

Although I didn't get paid for working at ORJ, I did benefit in ways that money couldn't buy. I learned the processes of grant writing and fundraising, and I gained confidence in my abilities as a speaker and teacher outside the prison setting. I also got an opportunity to practice my organizational skills during fundraising campaigns. Another invaluable benefit was that I met dozens of wonderful people who started out as business contacts and became my friends. More importantly, my job at the Office of Restorative Justice gave me somewhere to go every day.

In retrospect, being needed on a regular basis helped me make the transition from newly released prisoner to useful member of society. I strongly believe that everyone who is released from prison should be made to feel useful and needed as part of their re-entry process.

After the welcome home party is over, life can become a very lonely and scary place. Everyone who gets out thinks their first priority is to find a job, but the real need is to find somewhere that makes them feel useful and needed. I thought I was working for money, but later realized I was working to re-establish myself as a relevant member of the community.

While I was still inside I came to the conclusion that I would be setting myself up for disappointment if I made plans or set expectations for my life after prison. I had been away for almost a quarter century, so my points of reference were obsolete. I had no idea what the outside world would be like or where I would fit in.

During my time in prison I had read hundreds of books. I had written manuscripts, essays, plays, and poems. I had taken classes, and attended a wide variety of programs and seminars. If all my efforts had been focused toward a course of study, I would easily have qualified for a PhD. Since it was Prison Study, however, it held no particular value to the outside world.

I left prison searching for the place that exists for anyone with a passion for what they believe in. My passion is teaching that no matter where we find ourselves in life, God has placed us there for a reason… and the reason is always a good one, whether we can see the good or not.

Chapter Fourteen

The After Life

Living on the outside was nothing like I had imagined. It was infinitely better than my wildest expectations. Still, I had a lot of catching up to do. So many of the things people use and take for granted today that were little more than science fiction 25 years ago was a continuous source of surprise for me.

One of my most embarrassing moments was when I was walking down the street and I noticed an attractive young woman walking in my direction. She was smiling, so I smiled back at her. Then she said, 'Hi – what have you been up to?"

I returned her greeting. "Hi. I haven't been up to much. How about you?"

The young woman looked at me, frowned, and pointed at her ear. She had a device in her ear that I would later find out was a Bluetooth and she was talking to someone on her cell phone. I might have seen a Bluetooth on TV, but never in person, so the reality of Bluetooth technology wasn't something I had expected. Since then, I have been very careful to make sure that someone who is speaking in my direction is actually talking to me.

My first Metro bus ride was also somewhat embarrassing. I found out just how much it cost to ride the bus, but fortunately had the exact change. The bus pulled up and I got on with my money in hand – it hadn't occurred to me that I also needed to know where to put the money. So there I was standing with my bus fare in my hand looking around for something that looked like the money slot. The bus driver had to point it out to me. Fortunately, she didn't make eye contact, so I came away with minimal damage to my fragile ego.

For the most part I am blessed with a core group of friends who were right there showing me what I needed to know. My challenges were mostly in the area of technology. Cell phones, the Internet, video recorders—I couldn't absorb the changes fast enough. I don't feel so bad about not being proficient in any of these areas. I discovered there are a lot of people who, despite not having taken a 23-year timeout from the world, are as equally technology-challenged as I am!

Another big lesson I learned is God only lets us keep the things we appreciate. Maybe it's Divine Redistribution, but if we are not grateful for something we have, God takes it and gives it to someone else. Therefore, I'm grateful for everything and everybody in my life. My life may still not be exactly what I think I want it to be, but it is exactly what God wants it to be, and that's good enough for me.

I lost my life once, and by the grace of God found it again… in the last place I looked.

***

EPILOGUE

Faith is like training for an event. The more we train for the event, the farther we can go and the longer we can last.

One of my most recent faith-strengthening events came after my wife, Diana, and I were married. She had to go 3000 miles away to take a job on the east coast. The job market was horrendous in California at that time, so when this job offer was presented, we agreed that she should accept it and relocate temporarily to the Washington D.C. area.

We packed up all her belongings and put them in storage except for what she would need back East while I stayed with friends. One of the last things we did was to send her car ahead on a car carrier. We agreed that driving wouldn't be a good idea. Everything was set with only a few days left before she would leave.

Just prior to her departure she got a call for an interview with the County of Los Angeles for a position she had applied to some months earlier. Since she already had a job waiting for her in Washington D.C. she wasn't going to go to the interview, but I convinced her to go just for the heck of it. The interview went like most interviews go, ending with a thank you from the interviewers and the not unexpected, "We'll let you know". Three days later she left for the East Coast.

Legal issues kept me from leaving the State of California and going with her. She would have to go alone. So, we said our goodbyes at the airport and she was gone.

Over the next three months we talked every chance we got and she came home during the holidays for visits that were too brief. Then things changed drastically and the two-year contract term of her job was suddenly changed to less than one year and the opportunity for advancement or a permanent situation was no longer an option for her because of her term contract employee status.

As if matters couldn't get any worse, the bottom fell out of her living arrangement. She had arranged to live with a friend she'd known since her early collage days. They had been fast friends for decades and had gone through much of life's experiences together. Diana believed everything was okay with the arrangement until what seemed to her, out of the blue, she was told to pack up her belongings and leave. Her life-long friend suddenly didn't like the arrangement anymore and wanted her gone. Diana was out in the cold.

She called me almost hysterical, "Herb, Jo put me out"

It was 8 A.M. her time, but 5 A.M. on the West Coast. I was still half asleep and it took a couple extra seconds for me to compute what she was saying. Even then I couldn't believe it.

"Wait. Calm down. Tell me want happened."

She sobbed her way through the details of how Jo, this life-long friend, had conducted an unauthorized background check on me without telling Diana what she had done. The report she got back apparently was just enough for her to convince herself that my past posed some sort of huge threat to her and her family through my association with Diana. So, Diana had to go.

In an inexplicable rage, she went into Diana's room and shouted, "Get out! Get out right now!"

"I tried to talk to her but she was beyond being reasoned with, so I packed all my belongings into my car and moved to a hotel."

Then she asked me, "What should I do?"

Although I couldn't logically justify my response, either then or now, without hesitation I said, "Come home."

As the words left my mouth I was as sure of what I was saying as anything I had ever said in my life.

"But if I leave I won't have a job and we won't have a place to stay when I get there."

"But if you stay there you'll hemorrhage money until having a job won't be worth it," I countered.

"Just come home. We'll work it out together."

"Okay." She agreed without another word of protest.

What happened next was nothing short of a miracle. Diana resigned her position, loaded all her possessions in her car, and started driving the 3000 miles from Washington, D.C. to Los Angeles. We talked on the phone most of the trip, except in those impossible places with poor cell phone coverage. We didn't talk much about our plan because we didn't really have one past solving our challenge together.

As Diana was crossing through Texas, she got the call. It was about the position she had interviewed for with the County of Los Angeles before she left California, the one I insisted she go to. They called to offer her the position and asked when she could report for work.

Whenever I share this story people are impressed, but none as much as we were. We took a leap of faith and God caught us. God only seems to fail when we fail to trust in Him. In retrospect, I can't imagine an alternative to the choice we made. We had run out of options; our only choice was to believe that God believed in us enough not to let us fail.

AFTERWORD
THE IMPACT OF ONE PERSON

What follows are thoughts shared by inmates at Folsom State Prison who lived with and were inspired by Herb. Included here also are the thoughts and impressions by friends and colleagues Herb worked with in Restorative Justice upon his release from Folsom State Prison.

"His faith, unshakable; his smile, contagious; his love and dedication for helping others, infectious."

~ Greg G.

"It was tremendous to have had a friendship with Herb. His counseling and advice have been integral in my life and have had a profound effect on who I have become today. Heaven is a much better place because of the presence of Blake."

~ Tony C.

"All us who knew Blake knew the heartfelt pain he has been through over the years, how much he had grown and how much love he showed to all who were around him."

~ Lawley Sr.

"Having met hundreds of prisoners during my incarceration since 1997, I can say without reservation that Herb Blake is one of the very few people who was truly a 'blessing from above'. He was, and continues to be, a positive inspiration to all of us who believe in restorative justice."

~ Kenneth K.

"The Book says that there is a personality change sufficient to bring about recovery from alcoholism. Blake displayed this personality change."

~ Greg W.

"It's very rare for a human being to experience his or her dreams, but Blake came to realize the potential of his dreams. It is always miraculous to see a dream take shape and form. Dreams themselves are made of the chiffon of men's hopes, desires and aspirings. This is the first miracle: Blake became his dream; the second miracle appeared when he found his place among the particular facts of life."

~ Charles M.

"Blake, you were always a man of principles and of conviction. That was evident to all who knew you. What was even more profound, however, was who you were to those who did not have the privilege of knowing you: you were trust, love and comfort. You ARE forever in our hearts."

~ Kevin G.

"I can say he was my friend. We attended many self-help groups where I'd gotten to know him. From the first day we met to the last day I saw him, I considered him as one of my best friends."

~ Villalobos

"It is never easy waking your brain and finally coming to the realization that someone who has always been there is no longer. ... Sometimes people come into our lives for a reason or a season, and maybe for a lifetime. Blake fulfilled all three. ... After speaking with Blake, you knew in your heart that everything would be alright."

~ Mike-Mike "Tex"

"All people are born and then die, but very few truly live. Blake truly lived this life! My memories of him will always carry the emotion of joy. And from my point of view, he will always be an example of resilience and of what a true friend should be."

~ Elroy R.

"On Saturday mornings my wife and I attend a Catholic volunteer program at a Los Angeles Probation Camp called Camp Miller. It is located in the Santa Monica Mountains above Malibu, California. The camp houses boys ages 13 to 18 years old who have run afoul of the law. We felt Herb's book, *The Last Place I Looked*, was a story the young boys needed to read. Our church, American Martyrs Catholic Church in Manhattan Beach, California, provided the funds to buy 30 copies. The feedback we received from the boys was that the story moved them to think about the poor choices they had made in their lives. Along with the help of the director of the Catholic volunteer program at Camp Miller, we brought Blake to camp to speak to the boys. The connection Herb made with the boys was magical. They sat through his presentation with rapt attention. At the conclusion of his presentation he led the boys in a rousing promise to seek independence of gang life and the boys joined in with gusto. Many of the boys wanted to talk to him one-on-one.

For weeks after our church provided more copies of Herb's book. Herb's reaction to the positive feedback we gave him was like tonic for him. He beamed as he heard the therapeutic effect his book had on the youngsters. In the three years he lived after leaving prison, Herb tried to provide significant contributions to society. Any positive effect the book had on the boys' future attempts to be good citizens and contribute to the common good was a great a gift they returned to Herb.

He also touched our lives in a very special way and is truly missed."

~ Tony & Lynn Fadale

"I had the pleasure of meeting Herb in March of 2009, when he had only recently been back in LA. By the way he carried himself, and the sharp suit he had on, I guessed he was a judge or a trial lawyer coming to speak to our law school class. Of course, his credentials on speaking to Restorative Justice were as meaningful as they could get.

Through diligent attention to his own inner life and past life he had accomplished the alchemy of so much personal transformation. When I asked him how it was that he managed to be released from prison during a time in California when so few people were being let out he told me, 'When you're at a party where you don't belong it's only a matter of time before someone asks you to leave.' I've never forgotten that.

We became close friends for what unfortunately turned out to be the short number of years remaining for him. Through our friendship I was able to observe his passion, creativity and persistence in working to contribute to a societal transformation from a culture of punishment to one of healing and forgiveness.

Herb's own life on the outside was one of restorative justice. In the face of the adversities life; prejudices, competitiveness, the logistics of being under state supervision without state support, Herb forged friendships with the world that spanned the globe, built on responsibility, reconciliation and love. I am truly grateful to have been one of those friends and to now have the opportunity try and pass it along."

~ Seth Weiner

"I had the privilege to meet Herb Blake, who wanted to be called 'Blake', in 2008 at Folsom State Prison. He was dressed in prison blues and, according to our mutual friend, Ray, who introduced us; Blake was probably not getting out any time soon. His upbeat, friendly demeanor, bright-eyed, smiling, and warm surprised me. We made an instant connection. When he told me that he was from L.A., I replied, 'I live in L.A. When you get out, give me a call.'

To everyone's amazement, including Blake's, the court granted his petition a few months later. He was released on parole in December

2008. He called me when he got to L.A. In no time at all, Blake and I became friends.

Out friendship was all too short, only a little over three years. During that time, we had many long conversations, many about prison. The one that sticks with me was the one he told me about forgiveness. I think it defined his character. It went like this:

In 1986, Blake and his half-brother, Kyle, got into a dispute with a drug dealer in South Central Los Angeles. The dealer beat Blake's brother with a baseball bat and nearly killed him. Blake rushed him to a hospital. The next day, Blake returned with his brother to confront the attacker, to threaten him with a gun. Tragically, Blake ended up fatally shooting the man.

Kyle was arrested first; he confessed and gave the police evidence against Blake. When Blake was arrested, he discovered that his brother had snitched. At that point, he had no choice but to plead guilty. He was sentenced to 15 years-to-life, a sentence that stretched out to 23 years.

During the first several years of his incarceration, Blake harbored a deep and consuming hate for Kyle. He was obsessed with revenge. He probably experienced the worst effects of vengeance: 'Vengeance is like swallowing rat poison and then waiting for the rat to die.'

But God wasn't done with Blake. Over a number of years he took positive steps: he became a serious reader, learned to be an X-ray technician, participated in AA, NA and developed a spiritual practice.

But Blake's major break-though came when he made one of the most important decisions of his life: he decided to ask Kyle to forgive him.

Yes, not to forgive Kyle, but the other way around. Not only did Blake stop seeing himself as the wronged victim of Kyle's 'snitching', but he went deeper. He saw the truth of the matter. Blake had been responsible for involving Kyle in the crime. Blake had committed the murder. Blake needed to ask Kyle for forgiveness. And he did. He wrote an eloquent letter to Kyle.

I am convinced that this decision brought Blake home to himself; that humbly asking forgiveness was the last turn in a long road. Herb Blake went on to become the good man I met that day at Folsom in 2008."

~ Scott Wood

FINAL THOUGHTS

The night before Herb left Folsom prison for the last time, he gave the following message to one of the volunteers to share with his friends inside. It is as apt now as it was when he originally penned it:

Dear Friends,

For some time we have joked that I might not be here for the next meeting. Little did we know how prophetic our words were the last time we said it … I am scheduled to leave tomorrow morning, December 16, 2008.

I couldn't leave without telling you all how much you have meant to me. For the last ten years my life has changed dramatically by members of our Fellowship. I have achieved a level of awareness that I could only have found in the most unlikely spot on earth, Folsom State Prison.

I want to thank all of you for what you've given me. Each of you has contributed to my personal and spiritual growth in ways that you can never imagine. I will forever be indebted to you for your special gifts. Although I will not be here with you physically, my spirit will attend each group and my energy will merge with yours for our greater good.

I regret that I couldn't say goodbye in person, but this is not actually good-bye, but "I will see you another time in another place."

Much Love and Many Blessings forever,
Your spiritual brother,
Blake

ABOUT THE AUTHOR

Herb Blake was a well-known advocate for Restorative Justice and worked with Homeboy's Industries and Loyola Law School to educate the public about the importance of community involvement in the healing process of re-entry. Herb's motto was "Never quit."

Herb frequently facilitated or participated in Centering Prayer, Alternative to Violence, Anger Transformation, and other self-help programs. He believed it is everyone's responsibility to take care of those who can't take care of themselves. Most importantly, he taught that forgiveness is a gift from God that we are obligated to share with others as freely as God bestows forgiveness on us. Herb was passionate about Juvenile Justice Reform and he believed that it is everyone's obligation to see to it that our youth are given a second chance. He worked tirelessly to improve and bring Restorative Justice and Forgiveness Workshops to individuals and community-based organizations that worked directly with incarcerated and recently released individuals struggling to accept themselves and adjust to life outside the confines of prison walls.

Herbert D. Blake died peacefully on January 8, 2012 with his wife, Diana, by his side.

ABOUT THE EDITOR

 Diana Baumbauer, Herb's widow, continues his work as an advocate for Restorative Justice and community healing. She is currently editing and compiling the remaining body of work by Herb Blake.

An artist in her own right, Diana creates original works of art as tools in healing, spirituality and education encompassed by Restorative Justice.

Diana continues to live in Long Beach, California with their cats, Sam and Bianca.